PHANTOMS OF OLD LOUISVILLE

Ghostly Tales from America's Most Haunted Neighborhood

David Dominé

PHANTOMS OF OLD LOUISVILLE

Ghostly Tales from America's Most Haunted Neighborhood

by David Dominé

McClanahan Publishing House

10-digit International Standard Book Number   0-913383-95-3
13-digit International Standard Book Number   978-0-913383-95-7
Library of Congress Card Catalog Number   2006929105

Cover and Book Design by James Asher

Manufactured in the United States of America

All book order correspondence should be addressed to:

McClanahan Publishing House, Inc.
P.O. Box 100
Kuttawa, KY 42055

270-388-9388
800-544-6959
270-388-6186 FAX

www.kybooks.com

McClanahan
Publishing House

TABLE OF CONTENTS

DEDICATION

For Bess, a sweet little schnauzer and the kindest soul I know . . .
although she can get cranky when you wake her
from one of her frequent naps.

PREFACE

*A*s I stated in my first book, *GHOSTS OF OLD LOUISVILLE: True Stories of Hauntings in America's Largest Victorian Neighborhood*, I am not a parapsychologist and I don't purport to know what 'ghosts' really are. I don't even know if I believe in phantoms, specters, spooks, haints or whatever the supposed cause of perceived supernatural activity may be. I still think that individuals who claim to experience telekinetic activity, earthbound spirits, or whatever you want to call those types of phenomena deemed 'paranormal,' all too frequently attribute these strange occurrences to self-styled phantasms and would-be ghostly causes, rather than draw the most logical conclusions at hand.

If someone says his keys keep disappearing and reappearing in different parts of the house, it's probably due to *forgetfulness.* If you hear an unexplained creak or groan of the floorboards on a dark night alone in your bedroom, *that just happens sometimes,* especially in older homes. If the door just closed on its own, I'd say *the wind* most likely blew it shut. If you thought you saw something out of the corner of your eye, it might have been nothing more than a simple *shadow* or the result of an overactive *imagination.*

Now, on the other hand, if you see your keys rise off the mantel in the living room – of their own accord – and then fly through the air and land on the parquet floor in the hallway, it will most likely send chills down my spine. I don't have an explanation for that. And if you say you heard a strange creak last night and turned around to find a shadowy figure in mist hovering before you, or that the door kept slamming shut before your eyes – even after you propped it open with a stop – it will most likely give me the creeps. I can't explain those types of occurrences, either. These kinds of happenings are extremely rare, however, and even when people tell me that things like this have occurred, I don't always believe them.

One thing of which I'm, nevertheless, still certain is that people do experience strange and unexplained occurrences. Whether or not they can in fact be blamed on telepathy, mental energy, restless souls, residual views of the past or just plain imagination is something I don't know, either. But add a bit of thunder and lightning on a dark and dreary evening, and you've got the perfect makings for a ghost story. If you can add a spooky-looking old house where phantoms are said to lurk in dark corners or a bit of tragedy to the mix, *all the better.*

Old Louisville boasts hundreds of these slightly imposing, if not misunderstood, old houses. It teems with grand town homes and mansions with elegant front parlors where Victorians used to lay out their dead for wakes and vigils, and they all harbor shadowy corners where secrets and specters abound. And the more you talk about these phantoms of the past, the more they come to life, yawning and stretching, stumbling to the thin veneer of the present that is the surface of our reality, rattling their chains for attention. The tales in this book add to a collection of stories centered on events and places in the Old Louisville neighborhood in Kentucky, a Victorian gem that has seen its share of sorrow and splendor.

Given that I've tracked down over a hundred alleged cases of hauntings here, many have suggested that this neighborhood might in fact be *the most haunted neighborhood in America.* As is the case with so many other grand neighborhoods in this country, these ghostly tales form part of the collective memory and highlight the local history and flavor. As with my first book, some of the stories presented for you here appear as firsthand accounts of unearthly happenings, while others come as legends that have taken root in the area. Some have been documented before, while others make their first appearance in this tome.

And, as I prefaced in *GHOSTS OF OLD LOUISVILLE: True Stories of Hauntings in America's Largest Victorian Neighborhood,* I am not a historian, either. I'm just a curious individual – and writer – with a penchant for haunted places. I make no claims as to the veracity of the information herein and offer them for enjoyment only.

Another thing I am not is a *ghost hunter.* Yes, I do hunt down *ghost stories,* but that's as far as it goes. Although I occasionally do tag along on psychic investigations with the various paranormal research groups in the area, I do so as a mere observer, and I profess to have none of the scientific expertise – or common sense – that would enable me to conduct an authentic psychic investigation. I collect information and then write it down in story form; that's it. I'm not trying to convince anyone of anything (other than what a great place Old Louisville is), and you can choose to believe the accounts I have documented in this book, or you can shake your head in disbelief and move on to your next read. I don't care either way, but I do hope you get a couple of goose bumps as you read these stories.

I have conducted countless hours of research and interviewed scores of people, so these accounts do indeed have a basis in fact. As for the many people I interviewed, some of their names have been changed to provide anonymity, since it would appear that many fear ridicule and derision, even though they do not waver in insisting that these stories are true. When I quote an individual and mention the name, this indicates a firsthand source I interviewed. When I quote other individuals but do not give a name it is because the information is secondhand.

Old Louisville has more than its share of spooks and specters – rightly so – and it has been a pleasure *digging* them up. I only listened to what I heard in the front parlors of these magnificent homes, and sometimes in the rustling of the branches overhead. Old Louisville is a marvelous place, and all you have to do is open your eyes and take a really good look at your surroundings to realize that life is indeed full of mystery and wonder. I hope I continue to pique your curiosity and entice outsiders to come and explore our haunted lanes and alleys, hopefully discovering the charms of this unique neighborhood in the process.

David Dominé
Old Louisville,
October 31, 2005

FOREWORD

*O*ur first meeting occurred in the winter of 1995. An icy wind blew and billowed at the snow outside, but inside the Seelbach Hotel, it was warm. David and I had met in the Oakroom, where he worked as a wine consultant for the restaurant, and we quickly hit it off. We had both spent time abroad and shared an affinity for fine food and wine, local history and quirky antics. Not only that, he demonstrated a remarkable knowledge of potables and spirits and showed himself to be accomplished in all things humanistic – especially foreign languages, the culinary arts, and world history – as well. In this day and age, one rarely finds such signature diversity, and I found David to be a sort not too readily seen in our modern-day era. After all, it's not every day that you meet a world traveler in his 30s who has already lived in the Philippines, Germany, Spain, Italy, Mexico and Austria. He has a singularly cosmopolitan outlook, and when I discovered that he harbored a penchant for the supernatural and old houses, I knew we would become fast friends.

Not to overembellish, but David immediately reminded me of Abraham Van Helsing of Bram Stoker fame. I could envision him in the study of some grand Old Louisville mansion, holed up for hours on end while he pored over ancient manuscripts and piles of books with yellowing, dog-eared pages rife with dust and sneezes. Under the cloak of darkness, I would see him – blond mane whipped by the wind – traipsing over moss-covered headstones in remote cemeteries as he eluded the shadows and attempted to dig up the past and unearth a dearth of secrets. A leather satchel in hand, he would roam dank corridors and search out a bit of the past for those sorely in need of a good dose of history and a little excitement. David Dominé conjured up worldly visions of grand adventure and exciting thrills; he was not your run-of-the-mill American.

As time went on I joined David's inner circle of friends and neighbors – many of them academics and professionals – and more often than not he would host weekly gatherings at his home. A type of salon-inspired atmosphere evolved where there would be a meeting of both minds and wills concerning the questions on the table. During these impromptu thinktanks where stories, opinions and playful banter would be swapped and embellished, David would orchestrate the evening from the kitchen – much to the delight and anticipation of those lucky enough to be present. He emerged as a maestro of fresh baked breads, homemade desserts and exotic dishes with artful presentations that choreographed and guided these meetings to a restrained crescendo, inspiring all with his creativity and attention to detail.

It was when the wine ran low and the candles all but burned out that the conversation usually took a turn to the realm of the ethereal. It was during one such gathering in the wee hours of the morning that David first announced his intentions, his plan to bring to the light the purported supernatural happenings that had occurred in his own abode, as well as in those of his Old Louisville neighbors.

In David's first book, *GHOSTS OF OLD LOUISVILLE: True Stories of Hauntings in America's Largest Victorian Neighborhood*, the reader gets precious glimpses into the goings-on that transpired during these Thursday night gatherings. In *PHANTOMS OF OLD LOUISVILLE: Ghostly Tales from America's Most Haunted Neighborhood*, his second book, the tradition continues. As he suspected, his first book would strike a nerve, a very pleasant one, and the neighborhood has exploded with would-be paranormal activity. People have come out of the woodwork and have shared stories that remained dormant for years, inundating David with an appetizing tidal wave of ghostly tales and legends from this fascinating part of the country. Fortunately for us, he has decided to continue writing them down.

PHANTOMS OF OLD LOUISVILLE: Ghostly Tales from America's Most Haunted Neighborhood reveals more of this unique neighborhood known as Old Louisville. David has discovered that where there is history, there are usually ghosts and phantoms, and he has ingeniously figured out a way to use his ghost stories as vehicles for conveying history and sense of place. Like an archaeologist, he has patiently excavated a bit of the past and brought to light invaluable information that might have been buried forever by the sands of time. Having been a student of archaeology myself, I can appreciate his patience and dedication. He has declared Old Louisville his dig site, and using tools like pen and paper, he has set about to unearth a past populated by shadows, phantoms and lost spirits. It is a murky realm that teeters somewhere between the physical and the divine, an indistinct netherworld that balances precariously on the precipice overlooking what we call *reality.*

When I spent time at the Trappist Monastery near Gethsemani, I experienced a life that can best be described as *unexamined* at the very least. I sat at the feet of learned professors and scholars and had the opportunity as well to learn from holy men and women cloistered in mountain hermitages the world over. For some inexplicable reason, I have always felt a calling to align myself to such personalities, those individuals continually in search of the answer to the eternal question that plagues and blesses us all – Why? I have personally experienced events that affirm the position that the answer to this age-old question does indeed exist, and I relish the fact that someone dares to present information that makes us question our reality and purpose in life. It was no wonder that I found myself in the friendship of David Dominé, and now, ever so humbly, in this latest volume dedicated to his ongoing work. I hope you enjoy *PHANTOMS OF OLD LOUISVILLE: Ghostly Tales from America's Most Haunted Neighborhood* as much as I did.

Kelly Atkins
Louisville,
October 31, 2005

INTRODUCTION

*C*crisp fall day is indeed the perfect time to stroll the streets of Old Louisville; nevertheless, a leisurely walk under the stars on a warm, sultry evening – or under the umbrella of a rain-soaked spring day – can be just as enjoyable . . . and just as *spooky*. Granted, a bit of fog or mist swirling at the base of the wrought-iron gas lamps that line the streets – or a sullen cluster of darkish, moody, gray storm clouds overhead – will add that extra touch of Dickensian ambience to your saunter, but in "America's Largest Victorian Neighborhood" all you really need is a bit of imagination and a set of open eyes before the past comes alive, and spirits from long ago start to roam and cast a wistful pallor over the quarter. Even a snow-covered day in the dead of winter will set your nostalgic juices to flowing, evoking a time forgotten when horses, polished and lacquered carriages in tow, clip-clopped their ways over the icy brick and cobblestone.

The phantoms of Old Louisville – it seems – ramble the old lanes and alleyways at all times of the year, no matter what the weather or time of day. A clean blanket of snow serves only as a blank canvas upon which imposing Victorian mansions of brick and slate tower over manicured boxwood hedges, while painting the story of generations before. Trees that have lost their leaves can only rail their gnarled branches against the icy winds, taking only cold comfort in the fact that spring is just around the corner. When the tender redbuds burst forth in April, joined by the lilies-of-the-valley and the dogwoods, the winter cold still permeates the bones and the wooden beams and rafters that brace and buttress many grand old homes in the area, waiting only till the stifling heat of August sets in and compels it to loosen – albeit begrudgingly – its hold on the region. Before you realize it, however, the chill of October whips down from the North and spikes the autumn skies with fierce and fiery winds that refresh the night air and restore the spirits of those wilted by the summer heat, plucking at those curious strings that sinew their way down along their backbones and cause them to jump at the random popping of an ember in the season's first fire. When you're outside in the cold of early November, you might pass a weathered old gas lamp at just the right moment when the faint glimmer of dusk halfheartedly relinquishes the last of its day to night, your skin nervously aprickle at the hiss and click of the lantern coming on in frail defiance of the dark. This is the time that phantoms from the past start to drift along the streets of Old Louisville, and you might just make up your mind that it's your favorite time of year.

But, then you'll – no doubt – decide that the brittle days after Christmas when nutmeg and ginger still linger in the air mark your favorite time of year as you meander your way through a won-derland of white powder and catch an eerie shadow staring down at you from a gabled attic window all adazzle with the bright glare of winter. Or, you'll think the same thing when mint leaves start unfurling themselves from fresh green stalks that have pushed their way up through the damp earth along century-old stone founda-tions, tender shoots that the warmth of Easter has awakened from invernal naps, just in time to spice the drinks of Derby. You revel in the warmth of the afternoon as you bruise their innocent leaves and cool them with crushed ice at a butler's stand in the oak-paneled library, finally drowning them in bourbon as you gaze nonchalantly out through a leaded fleur-de-lis in the lovely Art Nouveau window framed by lilac and maple trees. You add a conciliatory dash of sugar – only as an afterthought – but a misty silhouette against the burled walnut of the mantelpiece distracts you, and – despite a fleeting sense of disconcertment – the peppery jolt of the julep quickly reminds you that Old Louisville is a wonderful place to be, especial-ly in May. The shaded canopy over the quiet boulevard of Saint James Court at the peak of summer, nonetheless, has its own allure, more than ever when you hear the cooling splash of the fountain as the dappled sunlight dances at your feet and causes you to forget the haunting murmur singing to you from the rustling leaves above.

But then again, there is something about fall . . .

When the wind picks up and carries the dead leaves aloft in a miniature whirligig of rust and yellow, you'll smell the orange of the jack-o-lanterns eyeing you suspiciously from their perches in front of elegant town homes and Victorian manses that have seen more than a hundred Halloweens. When the branches overhead creak and groan and rasp as they fight to keep the last of their leaves, you'll lift your eyes and watch as a somber shower of desiccated foliage cascades in differing degrees of slow motion to deposit its shriveled members in the next earthbound twisterette of withered blades and grass that will carry on in an unrelenting cycle from which there is no escape. A shiver will pierce your spine – not altogether too unpleasant an experience – and you'll suddenly realize what time it is when the gaslights start to click on all over the neighborhood and fill you with a delicious sense of anticipation.

It's the time when history rubs the sleep from its eyes and speaks, finally sharing its secrets, inviting you to explore the cavernous parlors, the ornate entry halls and hidden passages of an enchanted neighborhood that time *really* hasn't forgotten. It's a time when floorboards rumble and creak, when doors slam shut and etched-glass windowpanes vibrate and threaten to shatter. It's the time when the past whispers and cajoles and murmurs and begs for a friendly ear. It is fall, and in Old Louisville, it is always fall . . . and this is the time when phantoms start to wander the streets in America's most haunted neighborhood.

No one has told these immense homes of another era that they are archaic and outmoded, energy pits of inefficiency. They still believe they are the city's bulwarks, home to limitless families for limitless generations to come.

Gerald Toner, *Happy Ghosts*

MORE ABOUT OLD LOUISVILLE

*M*ore and more people keep discovering that Old Louisville is indeed a feast for the eyes, one of the most splendid residential neighborhoods in the entire country with a very haunted past. Some even claim that it might be *the* most haunted neighborhood in the U.S. A leisurely stroll along its tree-lined streets can transport a visitor back in time to an era when a man's home truly was his castle. Here – along the boulevards, avenues and alleys of Old Louisville – you'll find blocks and blocks of grand homes and elegant mansions, over a thousand in all, with architectural styles and stylistic elements of past centuries from all corners of the globe. Next to modest shotgun structures and simple frame homes, you'll find stunning examples of Victorian Gothic, Chateauesque, Richardsonian Romanesque, Italianate, Beaux Arts, Craftsman, Queen Anne and Georgian Revival residences tucked in alongside houses with eclectic bits of Victorian Vernacular, Arts & Crafts, Renaissance Revival, Art Nouveau and Tudor influences as well.

Old Louisville counts as the first historic preservation district in the nation to bill itself as "America's Largest Victorian Neighborhood," and this engenders fierce pride in the locals. True, several other historic neighborhoods may be larger in both area and the number of structures contained therein; however, no other district can claim such a high concentration of almost exclusively Victorian construction in such a confined area. In the roughly fifty square blocks that comprise modern-day Old Louisville, roughly 90 percent of the fabled old mansions and town homes emerged at the height of the Victorian Era, which spanned from 1837 to 1901, and they constitute one of the most brilliant collections of antique residential architecture in the country. Not only that, local craftsmen and builders constructed the vast majority of these houses from locally quarried stone and hand-pressed brick – a good indicator of the wealth of the city back in the day – that would ensure a rock-solid and enduring existence for those buildings lucky enough to escape the wrath of the wrecking ball.

Paranormal experts have said that this solid construction lends itself especially well to supernatural activity given that the massive walls and firm foundations retain energy and create a portal to otherworldly dimensions. The colorful mansions that dot the lanes and boulevards of Old Louisville count as more than just architectural specimens and residences with a colorful past; they act as visual reminders of a bygone era that collect and replay images that have imprinted themselves indelibly on the fabric of long-ago domesticity. Not only that, they serve as havens for ghostly shadows and denizens of the netherworld, those random spirits that prefer to lurk in the corners and under beds rather than venture out into the daylight and risk imminent discovery. After all, *there's no place like home*, and the mansions in Old Louisville have been home to countless individuals and generations of families that have known heartbreak, joy, sorrow and tragedy.

Old Louisville has emerged as a shining example of a National Preservation District, the third largest in the nation, and the largest purely Victorian district in the United States. A wonderfully preserved time capsule, this vibrant neighborhood offers just a sample of the beautiful architecture and styles of urban living that at one time defined city life in the United States. Thousands of people from all walks and stations of life call Old Louisville home, and they welcome visitors the whole year round. For information about tours of haunted Old Louisville, call the Visitors Center in Historic Old Louisville at 502.637.2922 or go online at *www.ghostsofold-louisville.com*.

Haunted Old Louisville

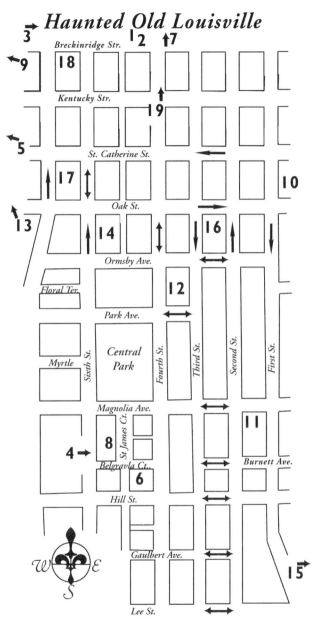

1. The 851 Mansion
2. Presentation Academy
3. The Monserrat
4. 1439 South Sixth Street
5. Twelfth and Zane
6. The Pink Palace
7. The Louisville Free Public Library
8. 1464 St. James Court
9. The Old Marine Hospital
10. 1135 South First Street
11. Alexander House
12. The DuPont Mansion
13. Union Station
14. The Speed Mansion
15. Farmington
16. The St. Ives
17. St. Louis Bertrand
    Catholic Church
18. The Seelbach-Parrish
    House
19. The Seelbach Hotel

Chapter 1

THE SPALDING MANSION

L ittle by little, word is getting out about this national treasure called Old Louisville, this somewhat remote corner of the world with its hundreds and hundreds of grand mansions and stately homes in the heart of Kentucky's largest city, this secluded time capsule from the Victorian era with its endless supply of stories and secrets. But, no matter how many books are penned about the colorful characters here, no matter how many years one resides here, it seems that new things can always be discovered. A hidden gargoyle of stone perched on a church tower, a unique turret hidden away behind a leafy canopy of maple, the tragic story of a prominent family's financial hardships, the sad tale of unrequited love . . . Old Louisville harbors scores of secrets – both inside and outside the solidly built walls of stone and brick that form the bodies of the staid homes that populate the neighborhood – and one only needs a curious attitude and a penchant for the undiscovered to get swept up in the past lives of this unique part of the world. But be forewarned: Old Louisville has been known to "swallow" people up.

A similar reference could be made about one of Louisville's

nearby architectural treasures, the lovely Thompkins-Buchanan-Rankin Mansion that my friend and colleague, Judy Cato, mentioned in the *Afterword* of my last book. One could say this lovely Victorian residence – also known as the Spalding Mansion or the 851 Mansion – has been swallowed up as well. Located just outside the actual boundaries of Old Louisville, this important local landmark remains largely undiscovered to even the most intrepid of local explorers – possibly because of its location slightly *outside* the Old Louisville Preservation District, but most likely because it remains totally invisible to passersby. Planners at Spalding University thoughtfully incorporated this elegant residence into the main building during the school's construction in 1941, and today the small liberal arts university envelopes it on all four sides. A fortunate twist of fate, it has preserved a rare glimpse into the glorious past enjoyed by Old Louisville in the 1800s, when so many other architecturally shortsighted ne'er-do-wells would have gone ahead and sacrificed the building to the tacky whims of the wrecking ball.

Granted, the lavish residence does come a block or two short of falling in the confines of the modern-day designation of Old Louisville; however, given the fact that the impressive structure can be said to be more indicative of the typical upper-class city residences that in their heyday dotted the *real Old* Louisville – that residential area between Broadway and Kentucky Street that housed countless shining examples of Federal and early Victorian domestic architecture – it certainly deserves inclusion in this book. This mansion epitomizes the grand age of residential construction that started to peak in the Derby City in the late mid-1880s when an influx of river trade and railroad travel inundated the city with an unprecedented degree of wealth. As Judy Cato said, "The Tompkins-Buchanan-Rankin Mansion is clearly one of Louisville's rarer gems," and it can only hint at the former grandeur on display in so many of the old homes that were offered up in the name of progress. Today it counts as a Kentucky Landmark and has been listed on the National Register of Historic Places.

Constructed in the Italianate Renaissance Revival style, it lays claim as one of the few remaining structures designed by architect Henry Whitestone, the preeminent regional architect of his day who left an indelible impression on the young architectural landscape of Louisville. Whitestone completed the mansion in 1871 for a local importer, Joseph T. Tompkins, who spared no expense when appointing the spacious interior rooms with the finest oriental carpets, hand-carved furniture, delicate porcelain vases and ornate light fixtures. In 1880, a local distiller, George Buchanan, purchased the property, and when he declared bankruptcy in 1884 and put the house up for auction, another distiller, Rhodes B. Rankin, purchased it. In 1918, the mansion fell into the hands of the Sisters of Charity of Nazareth, who purchased it and opened Nazareth College, the school that later became Spalding University.

Today, it forms the hidden heart of the university, a refined slice of the past tucked away in the entrails of the state-of-the-art institution where students can be found casually lounging on antique settees and davenports, or where the teaching body gathers for frequent receptions or department meetings. How many of them stop and ponder the past lives of this gentle giant known as the Spalding Mansion? How many of them give a passing thought about the previous owners as they trudge up and down the original hand-carved walnut staircase while sunlight filters down through the beautiful stained glass skylight overhead and illuminates the intricate walnut rosettes, florets and leaves in a comforting shower of blue, gold and green? One day I decided to find out, and the student I subsequently met – and whose story I heard – lead me to believe that some experiences in the old mansion can be anything *but* comforting.

She called herself Amber and refused to give a last name, saying only that she had recently enrolled in the university's creative writing program and that she hailed from eastern Kentucky. Tall and thin, with jet black hair and ivory skin that hinted at her Goth leanings, Amber and I had met on a steamy day in early spring when I had walked over to the mansion to snap a couple of photos with my digital camera. As with other stories, I hadn't actually dug anything up at that point, but I had the distinct impression that I eventually would.

Despite the heat outside, the spacious interior had managed to stay somewhat cool, and only a few students could be found inside; the regular term had ended and summer classes had just begun. As I had done on previous occasions, I tried to strike up impromptu conversations with those who weren't bothered that a complete and total stranger had approached them. To the contrary, most displayed a look of pleasant surprise when I informed them of my intentions of documenting – in some form or other – the history of the 851 Mansion. All of them – to my dismay – had precious little information they could share regarding encounters of the otherworldly kind in the lavish interior of the stately mansion at the heart of Spalding University. All of them, that is, until I met Amber.

She came across as a pleasant girl, if not somewhat aloof, and when I told her about my project, she informed me that she had already read my first book, eager to add that she was looking forward to the next. "I was wondering when you were going to get around to mentioning this place," she interjected between dainty nips at a raspberry snow cone. "There's a *lot* of activity in this place. I can feel it."

I asked her what she meant when she said she could *feel* it, and she gave me a bland retort: "I can *sense* those kinds of things, and I always have . . . I don't know how, but I just *feel* it, that's all. It's something you can't explain to someone who hasn't experienced it for herself."

We sat in the front parlor of the old home as we spoke, surrounded by high Victorian furniture. A long, rectangular room with a small bay to the north flanked by beautiful double fireplaces, its walls glimmer in gold-patterned wallpaper, and an enormous brass light fixture with numerous large globes and countless crystal prisms hangs from the ceiling. A masterpiece in and of itself, the ceiling – with its hand-appliquéd geometrical designs of ivory, turquoise and gold – accents the Art Nouveau elements in the room and counts as a stunning example of the importance upper-class Victorians placed on all aspects of interior design.

Amber quickly tired at my ignorance of her extrasensory abilities and decided not to "beat around the bush. If you're interested," she informed me, "some friends and I have been holding séances down here, and we've made some *interesting* discoveries." She raised her eyebrows and lifted her head in the direction of the dining room next door and smiled. "We're having one this evening, if you're interested. Be at the side porch at midnight, and I'll let you in." She quickly gathered up her things and left, not so much as another single word having been said.

I stood and half-heartedly considered the invitation, trying to keep an open mind in defiance of my skepticism regarding séances. Walking through pocket doors into the adjacent dining room, I observed a monstrously large sideboy of intricately carved wood towering against walls done in green and red when a sudden chill ran down my backbone. Enjoying the brief shudder, I realized my curiosity had been piqued, and I decided to make an appearance at that evening's show. I cast a glance at the large dining room table with its ornate centerpiece and eight high-back chairs in red upholstery and then left.

Eight hours later, I seriously reconsidered the idea of joining the festivities as I let myself out the back door and made my way through the alley behind my house and then down Fourth Street to the corner with Breckenridge. However, I reminded myself that I sorely needed some good information for the story, and I let desperation lead the way. As I approached the intersection and the fortress-like, red-brick, turreted structure known as Presentation Academy, I caught a fleeting glimpse of a shadow lurking at the base of the glimmering baroque-inspired limestone of the opulent Christian Church that sat across the street. *A homeless person?* I hoped it was nothing more than that and made my way through a back alley and into a series of maze-like pathways at the back of the main building. I ducked under a small Gothic arch and exited into a secluded courtyard.

Although the façade has disappeared, the exterior portions of the former Thompkins-Buchanan-Rankins residence still remain visible to observers, and the south-facing side of the Spalding Mansion loomed before me as the soft light of a solitary street lamp bathed the weathered brick and ivory trimming in a soft sheen. In the silent light, I glanced at my watch and saw that midnight had just arrived, a fact echoed by the lone peal of a tinny church bell off in the distance. My left hand tightly grasping what appeared to be a wrought-iron railing, I walked up the sweeping steps of the galleried, side porch and came to stand in front of a wooden door. I hesitated a moment and decided to knock softly, but before I had the chance, the door opened silently. Amber stood before me. "Good. You came." She said it matter-of-factly and pulled me inside, the door closing without a sound behind me. I decided to forgo the questioning as to how she had gained entry to the building at such a late hour and followed her through the dim shadows of the hallway.

We quickly entered the dining room, where four others sat at either side of the enormous table. In the center, a single large, ivory candle rested in a brass holder, while a bright orange flame flickered and danced about, its subdued light providing the only source of illumination for the assortment of somber faces in the cavernous room. "This is Peter, Marella, Christian and Jon," she said, pointing at the respective seats with a richly bejeweled index finger. Concluding her hasty introductions, she sat down at the head of the table and indicated that I should take the chair at the far end. I stammered a bit and tried to explain that I preferred to act as a spectator and not as a participant, to which she responded, "Suit yourself. You can still sit there and observe. This isn't the typical kind of séance, anyway, the kind where you hold hands and stuff." With an inaudible sigh of relief, I sat down and made myself comfortable.

As I looked on, it seemed that the group had gone through the same ritual many times before. Unprompted, they all closed their eyes and "cleared" their minds of negative thoughts for five minutes, upon which followed a sort of prayer in which Amber requested the spirits in their midst to cooperate or vacate the premises – or at least not interfere in their plans. She also assured them of her benign intentions and asked her "spirit guide" for protection during the séance. That completed, she stood and made her way around the table in a counterclockwise motion, pausing as she passed each participant to gently rest a hand on top of each head.

When she reached her own chair, she turned around and repeated the whole procedure in a clockwise motion, this time uttering a soft "amen" as she patted each head. After she rendered her last "blessing" and headed back to her chair, I noticed she had somehow acquired an object that she held out before her. She sat herself down – leaning forward in the process – and placed it on the table so it rested equidistantly from the five participants.

From what I could tell, it looked to be a large, etched crystal vase with a feather inside. I studied it a bit longer as she and the others seemed to pause and concentrate for a moment. The vase, an antique most likely, had a cylindrical shape and looked like it stood eight or ten inches tall. The white plume inside measured several inches taller than the vase so that the top portion of the billowy, downy mass stood visibly higher than the vase. Somewhat perplexed as to its significance, I studied the vase and feather a bit and then let my eyes wander about the rich appointments in the dining room as the others carried on with their ritual.

Overhead, the soft light of the solitary candle reflected off the glossy finish of the ceiling painted in a light turquoise, similar to that in the adjacent parlor. A band of pale yellow crown molding with dentils framed the ceiling and skillfully merged it with the elegant wall covering, and lengths of carved wooden trim had been applied to the ceiling so as to create a pleasant geometrical design. Only the barest hint of light could be seen through the two large windows that flanked the wall behind Amber, and it seemed that the rich burgundy of the draperies melted into the darkness. The stately mantel of carved wood with tiered curio shelves towered over the table and seemed to anchor the room.

I returned my attention to the séance and heard Amber take a deep breath. "Are you here?" she enquired. "If you are present, please let us know." To my amazement, the feather in the crystal vase seemed to raise itself an inch or two from the base where it rested, and then hovered for a second or two before falling back into the container, almost as if a slight breeze had caught it and borne it aloft momentarily. I tried not to act nonplussed as I observed Christian, the man to Amber's right, ask the next question. "Are you the same person we communicated with the last time we met? If so, please let us know." Once again, I stared in disbelief as the feather lifted effort-lessly out of the vase and hung, suspended by who knows what, before falling back inside. I tried to hide my discomfort as the others carried nonchalantly on. I paused for a moment and slowly turned my head both ways, trying to detect a draft in the room that might account for the feather's odd behavior. I could feel nothing except for the slow rash of goose bumps that ran up my spine.

Marella, the girl to my left, had the next question, and, like the others, she appeared to have her eyes closed. "Have you new information for us? If the answer is yes, please let us know." The feather moved a bit, then hesitated and danced an inch or two into the air before settling back into the vase. I slowly turned in my chair and tried to focus on the feather and its receptacle, curious to see if there were any discernible strings or wires or anything that could cause the plume to lift out of the vase the way it had done. I could-n't see anything at all.

To my right, Jon inhaled deeply, closed his eyes and said: "Will you tell us the year you departed this realm? If yes, please let us know." Almost as if on command, the feather quickly darted an inch or two upwards as the participants opened their eyes, and then it turned a graceful pirouette and dropped back into the vase. Peter, the one to the left of Amber, closed his eyes – almost in unison with the others – and then asked his question. "Did you leave after 1900?" If so, please indicate it to us." Unawares, I held my breath as I concentrated on the crystal vase. A few seconds passed, and noth-ing happened to the feather. Then Amber took over again. "Did you leave between 1870 and 1900? If the answer is yes, please let us know." The feather flew into the air higher than it had before, although it never came close to exiting the vase entirely, and then quickly fell back inside. I could feel my stomach churn a bit.

For the next five minutes, all the participants assembled at the table took turns asking what year the "date of departure" had occurred, starting with 1871 and patiently working their way up into the 1880s and then the 1890s. Throughout the entire proce-dure, the feather remained – motionless – in the vase. When Amber finally asked, "Did you leave in 1899?" and said, "If the answer is yes, please let us know," the feather quickly darted upwards several inches and landed horizontally on the table, next to the vase. "So, 1899 it is," affirmed Christian as he reached forward, picked up the feather and deposited it back inside its container. I involuntarily tensed for a moment, my knuckles turning white in the process, and let my eyes scan the room for reactions. Other than Christian, no one had made even the slightest movement.

Suddenly, all heads turned at the sound of several long notes issuing from the baby grand piano in the far corner of the adjacent double parlor. There were only three solitary tones, and it sounded as if an unseen hand had slowly pushed down on the same key three times in a row. Everyone hesitated, and I craned my neck to see if I could detect any movement in the shadows near the far-off piano. I could see nothing, save for the reflection of the candle light in a majestic, floor-length peer mirror trimmed with gilt that towered behind the piano. "It's doing it again," whispered one of the others. A knife of tense silence cut through the air. Again, three long, drawn-out notes resonated from the piano.

Instinctively, I shot up out of my chair and darted into the next room. Although darkness had largely shrouded the room in black, I could still discern the basic shapes and silhouettes of objects before me. In the second or two it took me to reach the piano, I saw nothing. At least ten or fifteen steps removed from the keyboard, the large doorway and adjacent hallway provided more light, but nothing could be seen there, either. Scratching my head, I returned to the séance table, only then coming to the realization that I might have upset the plans for the evening.

"Well, we might as well call it a night," said Amber somberly. "We won't get anything else tonight now." She looked at me as she uttered this last sentence, but I couldn't tell if she was angry or not. I hoped I hadn't acted inappropriately. I mustered an apologetic gaze and glanced at the others. "Sorry," I said. "I hope I didn't ruin anything. I couldn't help myself, I guess."

Amber reached over and collected the vase and feather, while the others stood and pushed their chairs back into place. "No big deal," one of them said. "The same thing happened last time, anyway. It appears we have a jealous ghost or spirit on the premises." I knitted my eyebrows in confusion. "When we make contact with our regular spirit, it seems that another one always butts in and messes things up," he clarified. "We use the feather as our instrument," he added, "but there's obviously another spirit who prefers a different instrument. Whenever we make any headway with our normal friend here, the other one gets jealous and starts banging on the piano. It has happened the last three times now." We all exited the dining room, sauntered down the hallway and out a back exit. Several minutes later, I was on my way home.

Fortunately, Amber didn't bar me from coming back for the next séance, and in the week leading up to it, I tried to do a little more research into the history of the lovely mansion at 851 South Fourth Street, which I discovered had originally been numbered 931. While rummaging through microfiched editions of *The Courier-Journal* at the Louisville Free Public Library, the past came alive as I came across this story from December 17, 1884:

> A big policeman stood at the door of No. 931 Fourth avenue [sic] yesterday and warned everybody who passed in to "keep your hands on your pocketbooks." The entrance was to the palatine residence formerly occupied by the family of George C. Buchanan. The occasion was the trustee's sale, at the public auction, of the costly furniture and fixtures.
>
> The crowd that gathered was notable for its elegance, large numbers and many ladies. Fully 500 thronged the hallways, blocked the staircases, and filled the parlors and reception-rooms, but the majority were present to satisfy an idle curiosity. It was a luxury to gaze upon the magnificent appointments. Nothing short of the most lavish outlay of means could have provided such a bewildering array of blended utility and artistic beauty.
>
> Even the coverings on the walls have been

made the subject of aesthetic study. This was shown in the new wallpapers, frequently designed to imitate metal, leather, majolica, delft and porcelain tiles. The wall ornaments, such as paintings, frames, plaques and statuettes, were in perfect keeping. The floors were richly carpeted, and variety, beauty and a perfection of finish was everywhere in the handsome polished wood appointments arranged in sections of various colored boards, yellow satin wood, white ash, yellow maple, buff oak and dark walnut. Holstery tapestries, damask curtains and portiers harmoniously contrasted with the wood finishings and wall-coverings.

The wall-coverings were made by Hegan Brothers, and are said to be the most elaborate of any in the Southwest, the cost of this work alone having been over $14,000. The side walls are covered with French *delicante papeur* of elegant design, while the ceilings and friezes are particularly fine. The library is papered with red bronze, with broad, hand-painted frieze and ceiling to match. The side walls of the reception-room are in green and bronze foliage, and the ceiling is in embossed red velvet laid in gold and picked out in transparent colors. The side walls of the drawing-room are in solid embossed gold paper, and the ceiling is beautifully frescoed. The dining-room walls are made to represent *old* tapestry designs, with the ceiling paneled in black walnut moldings, brass rosettes and hand-painted ornaments. Taken as a whole, the decorations are something simply magnificent, and as a specimen of the decorator's art, reflect great on the Messrs. Hegan. The work attracted great attention from those present at the sale.

The crowd began to pour in before 9 o'clock. The hour and a half which intervened before the auctioneer commenced the sale was devoted to an inspection of the furniture and equipments. Back and side entrances were locked and policemen were stationed at convenient intervals through the building to see that nothing unpurchased and not paid for was removed. From the first floor to the third, the visitors elbowed their way, stopping frequently to admire some striking article or ornate work of art.

An item which attracted more than passing notice was a group of 28 paintings, thirteen being the creations of Mr. Carl C. Brenner. Another noteworthy collection embraced 26 handsome and valuable etchings in bronze, the work of the late John Williamson. At 10:30 o'clock Auctioneer Sim Meddis erected himself on a table in the back parlor and commenced the sale. The auctioneer's outfit consisted of a huge pair of eye-glasses and a rolled gold watch chain. Mr. Meddis displayed a slight nervousness as he looked before him into an army of expectant faces. Almost every lady present wore diamonds and a sealskin sacque.

Among the bidders were: Mrs. R.A. Robinson, Mrs. John M. Robinson, Mrs. Garvin Bell, Mrs. Samuel B. Churchill, Mrs. Wesley Read, Miss Minnie Read, Mrs. Hampton Zane, Mrs. Henry McDowell, Mrs. Bland Ballard, Miss Walker, Mrs. Bonniecastle, Mr. M. Muldoon, Dr. and Mrs. E.D. Standiford, Mrs. Wm. Cornwall, Mrs. M. L. Clark, Mr. and Mrs. J. G. Coldeway, Mr. John Hancock, Mr. John DeWitt, Mr. and Mrs. Henry Heath, Mr. and Mrs. J.T. Gathright, Bishop T.U. Dudley, Rev. J.G. Minnegerode, Mrs. James Barbour, Mr. and Mrs. John H. Weller, Mr. C Henry Dorn, Mrs. J.B. Alexander, Mr. Joseph Brown, Mr. and Mrs. Cochrane, Mr. Julius Winter, Mrs. Allen Houston, Mrs. F. D. Carley, Mr. and Mrs. William Bridgeford, Mr. and Mrs. Flyshaker, Mr. and Mrs. Goram, Mrs. Quigly, Mr. and Mrs. Dennis Miller, Mr. and Mrs. Muir Weissinger, Mr. and Mrs. Beckley, Miss Lettie Robinson, Judge William Lindsay, Miss

Muir, Gov. and Mrs. Luke P. Blackburn, Mrs. R.H. Higgins, Mrs. W.C. Tyler, W. Chambers Taylor, Jr., Mr. John Stratton, Mrs. Hatton and Mrs. Eugene Elrod.

Just before the bidding began a sensation was created by the announcement that a lady had been robbed. Policeman Jacobs had a few minutes beforehand ejected two suspicious-looking characters from the residence. An investigation developed that the lady who had been robbed was Mrs. A. T. Smith of No. 636 Sixth street [sic]. The lady claimed that a pocket-book containing $15 and several valuable notes had been abstracted from inside the pocket of her cloak.

The bidding was not lively, but the prices realized were satisfactory, averaging about 40 per cent of the actual value of the original purchase money. It was amusing to note two diamond-decked ladies trying to outbid each other. Such sport was relished by no one so keenly as the auctioneer. He never missed an opportunity to excite the indignation of rival ladies, and make the winning bidder pay the highest price possible.

I also came across several photos of the Buchanan interior, and it appeared that little had changed since the splendid auction that had marked the decline of the Buchanan fortune. I could almost hear the auctioneer's gavel as it came down one last time in the opulent downtown mansion. I wondered if this sad departure from the family home had somehow triggered the paranormal activity that Amber and her entourage had tapped into.

Although my research had yielded no satisfactory explanations as to who or what could be paying supernatural visits to the elegant mansion on Fourth Street, I was looking forward to our next meeting, nonetheless. Once again, I met Amber and her friends at midnight on a Friday night in June, and it would prove to be an experience that I would never forget.

Tucked away behind the façade of the Spalding University administration building, a doorway leads into a veritable time capsule that preserves a slice of life from the Old Louisville of the 1870s.

The dining room in the lavish Spalding Mansion has played host to many séances over the years. An extremely popular pastime of wealthy Victorians, séances were used to make contact with the spirits of departed loved ones.

As before, Amber met me at the side door and let me in. She wore black again, but this time a large, gold amulet hung around her neck. I followed her through the dark corridor, and after exchanging cursory greetings with the others from the night before, I took the same seat I had previously occupied. The darkened room basked in the soft light of a single candle, and I realized how little must have changed in the house since the sad auction so many years ago. Amber commenced with her ritual, and I closed my eyes and envisioned the chamber full of elegantly dressed Victorians as they secretly gloated over the misfortunes of another.

A cool breeze on the cheek jolted me from my reverie, and my eyes popped open. The room had suddenly cooled, and I could see my breath as I exhaled. A rash of gooseflesh erupted on my arms and spread to my neck and legs. I glanced at the others and noticed that Amber was the only one who had managed to maintain her composure. From the startled expressions painted on Marella and Christian, and their rigid bearings, I could tell that this had never happened before.

Despite the uneasiness around the table, I could discern a faint smile on Amber's lips that gradually expanded to a complacent grin. She took a breath and then said, "Good. You are here. Are you the same as we met last time we were here? If the answer is yes, please let us know." All eyes stared at the vase and feather, and waited, focused. After what seemed an eternity, the feather stirred slightly and raised itself over the rim of the crystal vase. "Good," she replied with a nod of the head that indicated that Christian was to resume the questioning.

"Will you tell us your name?" the young man enquired. "If the answer is yes, please let us know." The feather shifted a bit, hesitated, and then catapulted into the air. One by one, the others took turns asking questions as they tried to discern the name of the entity present.

"Is your last name Thompkins? If the answer is yes, please let us know." There was no movement from the feather.

"Is your last name Buchanan? If the answer is yes, please let us know." The feather teetered back and forth a bit and then lifted

One of Old Louisville's best kept secrets, an impressive mansion attributed to local architect Henry Whitestone, hides behind the 1941 façade of the Spalding University administration building. Many believe this Victorian masterpiece to be haunted.

slightly. I wondered to myself if Mr. Buchanan really was paying a visit after all these years.

"Does your first name begin with an A? If the answer is yes, please let us know." The feather did not stir.

"Does your first name begin with a B? If the answer is yes, please let us know." The feather did not stir.

"Does your first name begin with a C? If the answer is yes, please let us know." The feather did not stir. It wasn't until someone asked if the name began with a J that the feather lifted itself from the vase in the middle of the table. Then they started all over from the beginning of the alphabet till they hit on the correct second letter of the first name. It was O. In another half an hour, they had worked their way through the tedious process of ferreting out the letters that would spell the individual's first and middle names.

Amber looked down at the notepad where she had jotted the letters and read the name aloud: "Joseph Rhodes Buchanan." She continued with a question: "Mr. Buchanan, did you used to live in this house? If the answer is yes, please let us know."

We all stared intently at the feather and vase, and nothing happened. Peter had just opened his mouth to ask the next question, when a sudden wind swept in from the drawing room. All heads turned and once again, the sound of several long notes issued from the baby grand piano in the far-off corner of the adjacent parlor. Again, only three solitary tones could be heard, and it sounded as if an unseen hand had slowly pushed down on the same key three times in a row. Everyone hesitated, and I craned my neck to see if I could detect any movement in the shadows near the far-off piano. Once again, I could see nothing, save for the reflection of the candle light in a majestic, floor-length gilded peer mirror that towered behind the piano. "What should we do?" whispered one of the others as the silence swirled about us. Again, three long, drawn-out notes resonated from the piano. This time, however, I made sure not to budge from my chair.

Amber kept her composure and asked another question. "If there is someone else here, would you like to communicate with us? If the answer is yes, please come to the table and let us know." In the silence, a clock could be heard ticking somewhere off in the distance, and all eyes trained on the crystal vase with the feather in it. Seconds passed and nothing happened. "I don't think it wants to talk to us," said Jon in a whisper. "Maybe we should just leave now." From the tone in his voice, it appeared that Jon had become genuinely nervous, a trait I hadn't noticed in him before.

Amber ignored his comments and sat, her eyes focused on the crystal vase. The candle sputtered a bit and sent a shower of shadows dancing across the wall behind her head. "Once again, will you communicate with us?" she demanded. "If you desire to communicate, please let us know." The candle flame continued its waxy dance as we rested our gazes on the vase and feather. It seemed that about half a minute passed, and then, the feather shot gingerly out of the vase and then settled back in. The temperature in the room seemed to drop, and we could all see our breath around the table.

"Will you tell us your name?" someone asked. "If the answer is yes, please let us know." Moments passed and nothing happed to the feather.

"He's obviously very stubborn," muttered Jon under his breath. "I don't like this at all."

"Will you tell us your name?" repeated Amber in a stronger tone. "If the answer is yes, please let us know." Nothing happened to the feather. "Do you still want to communicate with those assembled? If the answer is yes, please let us know." The feather stirred a bit and lifted out of the vase. Puzzled glances passed around the table.

"OK," resumed Amber, "Do you want to tell us something?" Before she had a chance to continue, the feather flew out of the vase and landed on the table in front of her. She reached over to pick it up, and then put it back in the vase. She looked at the others. "Let's do the alphabet thing, then."

Marella started. "We will each say a letter of the alphabet. If the letter is one you want to use, please let us know. Is the first letter an A?" she asked. "If so, please let us know." The feather did not move.

"Is the letter a B? If the answer is yes, please let us know."

The feather did not stir.

It wasn't until someone asked if the name began with an M that the feather lifted itself from the vase. Then, as before, they started from the beginning of the alphabet till they hit on the next letter. It was Y. Amber jotted each letter down, and they eventually worked their way through the monotonous task of spelling out the message.

Even before Amber looked down at her notepad and read the result, we had all managed to decipher the message. She read it aloud as we silently mouthed the words in unison: "MY NAME IS DARKNESS."

We all got up and left quickly without saying a word.

Amber invited me back to another séance at the 851 Mansion, but I decided I had seen enough. Still a skeptic, I've given up on trying to come up with rational explanations for the strange things I witnessed there, and have chalked it up to the 'unknown.' I'll forego any investigation dealing with the "My-Name-Is-Darkness" element from that night, but the very next day after the séance, I started researching possible connections with a Joseph Rhodes Buchanan who died in 1899. I was very startled with the information I found.

Searches at the Filson Historical Society and the Louisville Free Public Library revealed very little about the Buchanan family, and even less about the Thompkins and Rankin families. What family material I was able to unearth about the Buchanans made no mention of Joseph Rhodes Buchanan, and the trail quickly grew cold. I found it interesting to learn that the family home reportedly had been at one time a favorite gathering spot for neighborhood séances, many of them taking place at the large table in the *dining room.* Not only that, the Buchanan residence supposedly had been the scene of an authentic mummy unwrapping in the late 1800s as well. As a last resort, I decided to rummage through the clippings files at the library and see what I could find.

From what I could tell, it appears that the clippings files came into being in the 30s and 40s when an attempt was made to organize various newspaper articles dealing with the same people and topics. Hundreds of green cardboard file holders filled with brittle pages pasted with yellowing clippings line the shelves, and pulling out their contents is not for those with an aversion to dust or musty smells. I located a box with clippings from BRU to BY and delved into its dusty contents. About halfway through I pulled out a single, typewritten entry that had been pasted on a brittle piece of black construction paper.

It appeared to be an annotation from the *National Encyclopedia for American Biographies* about "Dr. Joseph Rhodes Buchanan, the noted writer upon medical and occult topics." The clunky letters of an old-fashioned typewriter also said that he had been born in Louisville in 1814, and died in California in 1899. One final bit of information noted that after his death, his brain was weighed (a common practice, I learned) and found to weigh considerably more that the average human male's.

Intrigued, I went to the Internet for more research and found out that Dr. Joseph Rhodes Buchanan, a respected American scientist, enjoyed some level of renown for coining the term "psychometry" or "the measuring of the soul" in 1842. He had strong Kentucky connections, but as for his relationship to the Buchanans at 851 South Fourth Street, that's not quite as clear. Amber and her friends will have to find that out at the next séance.

ABOUT PRESENTATION ACADEMY

The imposing, red-brick structure that occupies the corner lot to the south of the Spalding Mansion boasts a history as storied and colorful as any of those within the confines of the Old Louisville historic preservation district. Originally founded in 1831 by the Sisters of Charity of Nazareth, the illustrious institution has been an important part of the Louisville community since the very early days of the burgeoning city. The striking edifice that houses the girls' college-preparatory high school today has loomed over the corner of

Since the 1800s, generations of Louisville girls have attended the prestigious school known as Presentation Academy.

Fourth Street and Breckenridge since 1893, when local workers and masons began constructing its rock-solid foundations and thick walls. The architect, D.X. Hutchins, envisioned a stalwart Richardsonian-Romanesque bastion of learning where girls from the finest Louisville families would benefit from a solid education and the genteel art of finishing. Books in hand, countless numbers of young women have stridden its hallways during the course of their educations, and many pupils have at one time or other had the distinct impression that girlish wraiths of a bygone generation still loiter in the shadowy groves of academe.

"I was walking down the hallway to my biology class one day," remembers Mandy Sidell, a Louisville attorney who attended 'Pres' in the early 80s, "and I looked over to my right-hand side and saw this other girl walking next to me. It was strange because I thought, being late to class, I was the only one in the corridor, and I hadn't noticed her before. Not recognizing her, I assumed she was new, and smiled at her to say hello, but she just kept looking straight ahead. Then I realized she wasn't wearing the same kind of outfit I was wearing. Her skirt was longer, and she had a different kind of blouse on – kind of like from the 30s or 40s, I'd say. And her hairstyle was definitely not modern."

Sidell says her eyes wandered down to check out the new student's shoes when she almost had a heart attack. "She didn't have any feet!" she says. "Below the hemline there was nothing there at all! And then I realized I couldn't see arms either – it was just the main part of the body that was walking there next to me." Flustered, the former student says she stopped dead in her tracks and watched on in horrified amazement as the disembodied spirit slowly continued on her way down the hall and soon disappeared altogether. "She just faded away, bit by bit, and then she was gone!" she recalls. "And I had to walk into my biology class and act like nothing had happened, because I know nobody would have believed it!"

However, Mandy would have surely found a sympathetic ear or two despite her misgivings; it seems that tales of ghostly co-eds and eerie, shadow-like figures abound at Presentation Academy. Some even claim that the lost spirit of a former nun who fell down the stairs so many years ago still haunts the tragic spot of her demise. Not only that, many students have heard the legend of Mary White, a budding local socialite who supposedly met an untimely death in an automobile accident on the way to her coming-out party in the 1930s. Some claim that her body suffered terrible mutilation, and this purported maiming can account for the absence of limbs whenever girls spot her.

Although several Pres students reportedly did die in car wrecks in the pre-WWII years, no historic evidence has surfaced that can substantiate this rumor. But, as is the case with so many stories in Old Louisville, blurred memories of the past and lack of proof can hardly discredit what many consider the truth, and local legends still linger, hovering over the fine line between fact and fiction. Real or not, Mary White has been locked in limbo, her sad specter still haunting the hallways of her alma mater, joining the ranks of so many memories that make up the storied history of one of Louisville's most prestigious schools.

ABOUT MUMMY UNWRAPPINGS

When the young Queen Victoria started her reign in 1837, the United States had already wrested its independence from Great Britain, and Louisville had started to inch its way to the 50th anniversary of its founding by adventurous French and English pioneers. Like most American cities, the young river town would continue to look to the mother country for guidance in all things dealing with fashion and society well on into the next century. When Victoria died in 1901, she had become an icon in this country as much as in her own, and Victorian America would emulate all things British for years to come. Like their counterparts in other parts of the nation, Kentucky's upper-crust Victorians practically swooned at the notion of anything English and aristocratic, but in Old Louisville, these sensibilities were especially pronounced given the fact that the new subdivision they settled in the late 1880s incorporated posh London street names and locations to entice reluctant city dwellers to relocate. Evocative place names like St. James Court, Belgravia Court, Fountain Place, Victoria Place and so on served to replicate a bit of English refinement – even if in name only – in the heart of big city Kentucky. London society dictated many of the standards for local style and etiquette, and all eyes looked east to see what the next craze from England would bring. It hardly comes as a surprise, then, that when these image-conscious, would-be Bluegrass sophisticates got wind of the British practice of mummy unwrapping parties, they – of course – had to start hosting their own.

Nineteenth-century Victorians shared a particular fascination for exotic cultures – especially those of the Orient and Middle East – and amateur archeologists could be found sifting through the desert sands of alluring countries like Egypt where they hoped to uncover lost tombs and the ruins of fabled cities. Mummified remains popped up with such frequency that many would-be treasure seekers complained about them and viewed them as little more than bandaged nuisances. People actually burned them on large bonfires or used them to fuel the engines of locomotives at one time because so many mummies kept surfacing. British aristocrats – ever in need of new forms of diversion and entertainment – often impressed their guests by acquiring one of these gruesome oddities to unwrap at lavish gatherings and dinner parties. The popularity of these occasions grew, and curiosity-seekers could purchase tickets to these "unwrappings" that often took place in auditoriums for hundreds of onlookers. Although no self-respecting scientist today would condone such practices, they provided invaluable information about the process of mummification, and this, in turn, eventually led to a greater appreciation of Egyptian civilization and increased scientific interest in studying ancient remains.

At least two supposed mummy unwrappings took place in the Old Louisville neighborhood, one of them in the elegant parlor or dining room of the 851 Mansion at Spalding University. Accounts vary as to how the host conducted these unwrappings, however. Oftentimes, onlookers merely observed in morbid fascination while the unwrapper painstakingly deconstructed the mummified remains and shared his discoveries with the crowd. On other occasions, it seems, those assembled treated the unwrapping as an actual game. For these macabre soirees, a person would be chosen to "start" the mummy unwrapping, and he or she would undo the piece of bandage he or she had grabbed until it broke or disintegrated, upon which the next player would take over, and so on, until the "winner" removed the last piece of cloth, thereby winning the prize, whatever that happened to be. (Given that some mummies sported hundreds of yards of linen bandage, one would have to question the stamina of these party-goers.) In any case, elegantly dressed butlers served cocktails during the ordeal, and invitees enjoyed a lovely eight-course dinner where they shared their knowledge of – and fascination for – the ancient lands of the pharaohs and date palms.

Chapter 2

THE MONSERRAT

Like the lovely mansion hidden away at 851 South Fourth Street, the Monserrat counts as an Old Louisville landmark, even if it does fall outside the technical boundaries of the current-day Old Louisville neighborhood. Constructed in 1857, this stately, red-brick structure at the corner of Fifth and York presents a modestly regal façade that survives as one of the oldest buildings in the city. In the *Encyclopedia of Louisville,* contributor Robert Bruce French explains that architects Henry Whitestone and Isaiah Rogers designed the Italian Renaissance Revival building with 9-foot-tall, rounded-arch windows to provide maximum light for the spacious classrooms. Originally conceived as a school house, the Fifth Ward School replaced an older structure that had occupied the spot till a fire destroyed it in 1854. Although the Union Army appropriated it for use as a hospital during the Civil War, it eventually resumed its role as a schoolhouse and in 1900, acquired the name "Monserrat" in honor of its deceased principal Laura Lucas Monserrat. Declining numbers finally led to it shutting its doors to students at the beginning of World War II, and government officials converted the venerable old structure to a dormitory used by soldiers on leave from nearby Fort Knox.

It gained fame in the 70s and 80s as the Natural History Museum of the Louisville Free Public Library, and, thereafter, it began its current phase as an upscale residential building. Although it has been converted to fashionable apartments, many Louisvillians still refer to it as the "old museum," and generations can still remember afternoons spent there, transfixed by the disconcerting gaze of the museum's star attraction: Tchaenhotep, the old mummy.

Even if the mummified remains of this ancient Egyptian have relocated to a different home at the new museum on Main Street, many still feel that the spirit of death still lingers on in parts of the formidable old edifice. Not only that, ghosts and apparitions seemingly abound, imbuing the old place with a decidedly haunted air. It would appear that some of these revenants from the afterworld haven't quite detached themselves from their former lives in the Monserrat.

"I always felt there would be ghosts in that old place, especially when I learned the interesting history behind it," remarks Annie Crabapple, a lifelong Louisvillian who called the Monserrat home for most of the 1980s. "So I wasn't at all surprised when I actually saw a ghost one day." Crabapple claims she had a strange visitation that caused her skin to bristle with anxiety one cold December evening as she baked Christmas cookies to share with her neighbors. "I turned around and saw this little black girl standing there," she explains, "and it like to gave me a heart attack. It startled me, but it didn't scare me, if you know what I mean. At first, I assumed I had left my door open and that she had just wandered inside, but when I took a closer look, I could see that she wasn't real!" According to Crabapple, the figure appeared to be five or six years old. "And she was scared, I could tell that much. She looked out of place, too, because of the clothing she had on. No one wears tunics nowadays, and that's what she was wearing." Annie Crabapple claims the apparition lingered for another five or ten seconds, and then it slowly started to fade before vanishing altogether.

Although other manifestations, including those of Civil War

The Monserrat, an elegant apartment building at the corner of Fifth and York, was originally built as a school in the mid-1800s. Locals claim the basement harbors ghosts from when it was used a stop on the Underground Railroad.

soldiers, have occurred in various parts of the Monserrat, it seems that the sad figure of the little black girl has been the most prevalent. One former tenant claims that he witnessed the same apparition on no less than three different occasions, and each time he had the distinct impression "that it was a young slave girl who was sad about something." According to Ron Pettigrew, this former resident, these visions always appeared to him in the basement when he would go down to retrieve various items from storage. "One year I went down to the cellar to put my Christmas tree away," the fifty-year-old accountant recalls, adding that "it's a very dreary and dank place that will give you a bad case of the willies if you're not prepared for it. So I went down there and was putting my Christmas stuff away when I get this weird feeling going up my back, like somebody is watching me. So I turn around, and there's this little girl staring right back at me." According to Pettigrew, she could have been five, six, or seven years old and she wore a simple, bag-like dress and no shoes. "She just stood in the corner and looked at me with these enormous, sad, brown eyes. I think she was scared."

The next time Pettigrew had a visit from the young girl, he reports a very similar experience. "I had been down there several times since the first time I had seen her, and even though I kept an eye out for her, I hadn't seen anything, so this one time when I went down there I wasn't really expecting to see her. But, I turned around after setting some boxes down, and there she was again . . . just like the time before." Pettigrew says the apparition remained motionless and silent as before, and she also wore the same terrified look as on the previous occasion. "That was when I realized that she wouldn't appear when I was looking for her," he explains. "From that point on, I tried not to expect her when I went down there, but that's hard to do, telling yourself what to think. It only happened just once that I went down there without even thinking about her, and *that* time I saw her again, just as I had the two other times. I moved out of the Monserrat not too long after that, so that was the last time I saw her. But I'm sure if I went back there I'd see her again."

Although she herself has never experienced any ghostly visitations during her residency at the Monserrat, jazz singer Sandy

Neuman reports that she has nonetheless had some very strange sensations when she has found herself in the eerie and cavernous basement that lies beneath the venerable old structure. Neuman moved into her spacious apartment on the second floor in 1980, and since then she has become somewhat enamored of the austere, old building and its storied history. The basement holds a particular allure for her, and she has allowed herself to delve into the past lives of the gentle giant overhead.

"This was a stop on the Underground Railroad at one time, and they supposedly hid escaped slaves down here in the basement," she says. "When you go down there, you can see why it would have been a good place to hide people. It's very eerie." Although no documentation exists to support such a claim, many feel it wouldn't be entirely implausible for such a thing to have happened. For many runaway slaves, Louisville represented the last stop before crossing the Ohio River and entering the free state of Indiana. Little did they know that entrance into a Northern state did not automatically ensure safe passage to a life of freedom. The Hoosier State actually passed laws cracking down on fugitive men of color, and as a result, large numbers of escaped slaves crossed into Indiana and eventually found themselves heading back south.

"It must have been a terrible feeling to get all that way and get captured and sent back to their masters," says Hortensia Litton, an octogenarian whose older sister taught in the old building back in the 1930s. "It was still going strong back then," she recalls, "and my sister just loved it. Even back then it was a neat old building with a lot of history. We lived right next door, and she always used to spend a lot of time there after the students had left." According to Litton, her sister and her friends especially liked to conduct séances in the old Fifth Ward School. "Oh, back then séances and such things were ever so popular," she says, "and we were always getting together with friends and would always scare ourselves to death. It was a grand time. People don't do that so much nowadays."

Although Litton readily admits that her memory has faded somewhat over the decades, the alert woman says she recalls a particular evening back in the 1930s when her sister returned home after a night of 'sittings' in the old schoolhouse. "Oh, she was quite shaken when I saw her," she says. "She didn't dare tell mother and father what the matter was, because they were rather strict and did not approve of such things, but as soon as they had gone off to bed, she told me what the matter was."

According to Litton, her older sister had confided that some strange and terrifying events had transpired during the otherwise predictable séance. "She said that at first it was just like all the other times they had assembled to hold a sitting. They tried to get the table to move, and they would use a water glass turned upside down to spell out messages from the other side. Nothing much ever really happened." But all the other times hadn't been on a night of the full moon.

"My sister told me they were curious to see if a full moon would change how things went, and they decided to hold a séance at the exact minute that the moon achieved its completeness that night." Litton says her sister would never attend a séance again after that night.

"I remember her telling me how they could feel something in the air that evening. She said that the air felt electrified and like everything was full of energy. The moonlight was so bright that it lit up the room like daytime. That's what she said." According to Litton, her sister had experienced a strange sort of premonition as soon as she sat down at the table as well.

"It was like she was overcome with a sense of foreboding, she said. She told me she became really anxious all of a sudden and wanted to leave, but all the others just started laughing and teasing her, so she stayed put. But she knew something was going to happen because she could feel it in the air." Litton says her older sister described it as an "angry presence" in the room. "She knew there was something there because she could feel it."

As soon as the participants sat down at the table, they could feel it, too. "My sister said the first thing happened when they all asked any spirits in the room to give them a sign. No sooner had they finished the sentence when a whole bunch of books went flying off of a nearby shelf and scattered themselves all about the floor.

Then the windows started rattling so hard they thought they were going to break." After that, a strange, glittery haze started settling in around the table and spread out from them so they were all enveloped in it. According to Litton's sister, the fog had an odd, shimmering glow to it that made her heart skip a beat. "She said she was scared to death and didn't know what to do, so she just sat there and waited and watched. It was like this haze was full of all these little, tiny, tiny pinpoints of light that darted about and sparkled."

From the table, the eerie mist expanded and moved slowly across the room to the bank of large windows along an exterior wall. "The windows had started to rattle again, and the others were starting to get nervous now, too. But, then it got really still all of a sudden, and the haze started to get brighter. That's when they saw the ghost."

Illuminated by the bright glow surrounding her, a young, black girl clad in a formless smock or dress glowered at those assembled. Suspended a foot or so above the floor, the apparition remained motionless for a moment or two. "My sister said it seemed like forever, but it couldn't have been more than 30 or 45 seconds. She speculated that the girl had to be under ten and that it must have been an escaped slave girl from way back when. And she looked upset about something. I guess I would have been upset, too."

At that point, the windows started rattling and shaking again, and the otherworldly visitor suddenly faded and disappeared. "The weird fog just closed in on itself and got smaller, and then all of a sudden, it was gone. Just like that. My sister said they all just looked around at each other and couldn't believe their eyes. Such a strange sight! After that, my sister never attended another single séance in her life. That one was enough for her, she always said."

ABOUT SÉANCES AND SPIRITUALISM

Although society in Victorian America usually looked to England for inspiration and guidance, there were cases in which innovations that originated in the U.S. made their way to the British Isles. One of these took Europe – England especially – by storm in the mid and late 1800s after a pair of sisters from upstate New York made some startling allegations that would set the religious world on its ear. According to the Church of the Living Truth, on March 31, 1848, a remarkable and misunderstood movement known as Spiritualism came into existence, and it would either baffle or annoy all who came in contact with it. In the backwoods hamlet of Hydesville, New York, the spirit world supposedly announced its arrival through Kate and Margaretta Fox, two sisters who purported the ability to communicate with a phantom peddler named Charles Haynes who had been murdered and buried in their basement years before. The ghost reportedly employed mysterious rapping noises that apparently ensued from the floor and the walls to communicate with the young ladies and even gave the horrible details of his own murder. When someone later found actual human remains under the basement floor, the news spread to surrounding areas and eventually around the country where stunned. Others soon started claiming that they possessed the power to communicate with spirits as well. The modern phenomenon of spiritualism had arrived, ushering in an age of wonder and skepticism, and the world would never be the same.

Spiritualism – the belief that spirits of the dead communicate with the living through the use of sensitives known as mediums – relied on *séances,* a French word meaning sittings or sessions, to make contact with those in the afterworld. Participants would gather around a large table and hold hands while the medium attempted contact with the dearly departed in their midst. When contact had been achieved, those assembled would often hear mysterious rapping noises or unexplained voices from beyond, sometimes accompanied by levitating objects, ectoplasm or disembodied body parts. Typtology, or the unexplained tipping or raising of pieces of furniture and other heavy objects, evolved from the phenomena witnessed at early séances and continues to be an integral part of bona fide séances today.

As can be imagined, these claims of communicating with the

deceased caused quite a stir in the skeptical scientific world and incurred the wrath of many religious fanatics who considered it something akin to heresy. By the end of the 19th century, Spiritualism had suffered numerous blows to its credibility, including a confession by the Fox sisters in 1888, who claimed that they had staged the entire episode as a prank. Debunkers exposed many so-called mediums as frauds, and the entire movement suffered as a result. But, despite the countless numbers of fake mediums who exploited the bereaved and gullible, séances endured as a popular pursuit during the Victorian and Edwardian eras, and well on into the first half of the 20th century. Most, however, came to view the séance as a quaint, albeit outdated, parlor game that allowed those present to dabble in the forbidden world of the occult.

In Old Louisville, however, séances never quite lost their appeal, and many would gather around tables in elegant front parlors or grand studies so they could indulge their penchants for communications from the nether regions. If they couldn't round up an area medium of repute to sit for them, they'd employ the services of one of many local gypsy girls who claimed to have the "gift of sight," or else they'd chose a would-be seer from their midst and have him or her conduct the session. A prayer would be said, such as the following invocation from *The Spirit Speaks! Weekly Newspaper* of 1901, and then the séance would begin.

There is a land where we all go,
Whence ne'er the frost nor cold wind blow,
And friends remembered reunite,
And those who hate, forget their spite,
In glow surround these gentle beings,
We call you now to bless our meetings,
Heaven's promise, our spirits thrive,
So now for the living, let the dead come alive.

Greetings spirits,

Speak thee to us?

With a solitary candle on the table before them, those assembled would join hands and ask for messages from the Beyond. Sometimes so-called spirits would speak through the medium, other times they would cause various items laid out on the table, such as horns, hats and drums, to raise themselves and float in the air before the mesmerized onlookers. Some claimed to have received actual physical visitations from departed loved ones, and others would receive mysterious messages written in a familiar hand. Some communiqués came from dead relatives and friends of those present; others came from random, famous Kentuckians like Abraham Lincoln and Casey Jones. Celebrated Louisvillians like Jim Porter, the Kentucky Giant, and Sallie Ward also reportedly made appearances at several local séances held in Third Street mansions around the turn of the last century.

Old-timers in the neighborhood still talk about a legendary trance medium known as Madame Zanskaya, who in the late 1800s supposedly enthralled crowds of Louisvillians with her psychic abilities. Begarbed in flowered shawls with fringe and billowing red skirts that smacked of the stereotypical gypsy attire, Madame Zanskaya exuded an aura as mysterious as the spirits she ostensibly had the power to summon. On one occasion, while conducting a séance at the home of a wealthy Fourth Street tobacco baron, she supposedly caused an enormous table to lift off the ground and rise two feet into the air; when it started to tilt to one side, the stunned spectators observed in amazement as the candle and the other random items that littered the table top remained in place and refused to slide off the surface, apparently defying the laws of gravity in the process. One startled onlooker supposedly reported that the flame on the candle, however, remained in its original vertical position, maintaining its perpendicularity throughout the entire ordeal. By the time the weighty piece of furniture resumed its place on the floor, two women had allegedly swooned, and the self-proclaimed skeptic in the group – several shades paler than before – had acquired a newfound appreciation for the art of the séance.

Chapter 3

1439 SOUTH SIXTH STREET

usan Shearer is part of that rare group of individuals who have decided to make a significant contribution to the preservation of American history. She has – despite the inordinate amount of inconvenience, discomfort and expense – purchased a 115-year-old home in Old Louisville and has dedicated all her money and energy to a historic structure that might have languished to nonexistence were it not for her passion for antiques. "I got my first antique years ago," she recalls, "and after I got my first piece, I was hooked." It seemed only natural, then, that she would purchase an antique home in which to house her collection of antiquities later on. Little did she know that the cozy, little 1891 Queen Anne house at 1439 South Sixth Street would come with its own assortment of odd, paranormal occurrences.

Susan, an energetic insurance agent with four cats, says she purchased the house on a whim in 2003, after deciding to fulfill her lifelong dream of one day owning an old home with a fireplace. "I picked up the paper one day, and there wasn't anything interesting in the real estate section, so I decided to go and check out Old

Louisville." She drove from her home in the south end and found herself in front of the weathered frame structure at 1439 South Sixth Street. White paint had started to peel away in strips, and it appeared that years had passed since a human hand had tended to the yard and front walkway. A compact, two-story structure, the dwelling had nonetheless retained much of its original charm despite its neglected appearance. An inviting front porch welcomed visitors to the front door, and stained glass in a diamond-shaped window in a bay to the left and over the large picture window that overlooked the front yard hinted at the home's former grandeur. A picturesque turret at the roofline added an extra bit of enticement to the visage. Several weeks later, it belonged to her.

"I got a restoration loan," Susan explains, "and the bank had strict stipulations as to how much I would have to invest in the home's restoration. That's when the money started pouring out." The once grand lady had definitely seen better days, and Susan started to question her sanity as she took stock of the property she and her sister, Linda Gregory, had just acquired. "It had been divided into four apartments," she remembers, "and the back part of the building was actually crumbling apart." She knew a lot of hard work and patience would be required, but she had no idea just how much. A year later – just as her budget neared depletion – the house had been stabilized, and most of the major work like replastering and the tearing down of walls that were added at a later date had been completed. "Now, I'm at the point where I can start decorating, and that's exciting," Susan says. "I can't wait to get started!"

The exterior now sports a fresh coat of paint that attractively accents the muted blues and creams that highlight the home's painted-lady potential, and all that remains is to put on the final touches. Susan doesn't think it will take much longer to return the quaint residence to its former splendor, and she says she feels fortunate that the old house has chosen her as its custodian. She also hopes that the ghost of the little girl on the stairs likes what she does to the place.

"I don't know if I was exaggerating at first," Susan says, "but odd things just kept happening, and I started to get the feeling that something was trying to let me know that I wasn't here alone. And I just couldn't explain it all away with coincidence. I could *sense* something." These feelings of unease had started to plague her months before the misty apparition of a young girl in a white dress showed itself on the front stairs. What started out as random strange noises and odd occurrences quickly established itself as a series of unexplainable events with a pattern. Susan says the first happenings that made her stop and think involved the strange knocks she would often hear at the front door. "Usually around dusk I would hear three knocks on the window glass in the front door; and at first I didn't think anything of it," she explains. "Then after it started happening often enough for me to take note of it, I started waiting for it. Whenever I went to the front door, there was never anything there."

Susan recalls how she – on several occasions – went to the front of the house just as night fell and waited patiently to see if unseen hands would produce a knock at the window in her front door. "And sure enough," she says, "I would hear distinct knocks right on the glass in front of me, but I couldn't see where the raps were coming from, and I know nobody was outside." Susan had the windows checked, and they appeared to rest snuggly in their frames, so she claims there is no explanation for the series of odd knocks that she would hear only as sunlight faded at the end of each day.

The next strange occurrences to disconcert her centered around the radio she would listen to as she worked away on one of the many restoration projects that kept her occupied for the first year she was in the old house. "If I walked outside for something and left the radio on," she laughs, "it would be off when I came back in. And if I turned it off before I left, it would always be on when I came back." Susan says she would pay extra special attention to whether or not she turned the radio off as she left the house, and when she returned, the radio would invariably not be in the on or off state as she had left it.

Susan then remembers how little things started disappearing every now and then. "And it wasn't like I had misplaced anything, because I know that happens now and then, but it was different than that. It usually involved things I had more than one of," she explains. "For example, one day I had gone out and bought four new smoke detectors. I came home from the store and set them down, still in their bag, and when I went to get them later, there were only three!" Susan distinctly remembers bringing four of the devices home, and she had the purchase receipt to prove that there had been four. She says the same thing happened when she went out shopping one day and came across two small crystal lamps that she had to have for a downstairs powder room. "I got them home, and when it came time to put them out, there was only one there, and I had seen both of them a short time before." She also says no one who could have taken the items had entered the house, either. At least the house has a ghostly thief that is somewhat considerate. It could have taken *all* of Susan's items.

Another item to disappear, the picture of a young girl, made her stop and analyze her surroundings as well. "Workers had found a small photograph of a young girl in white near the mantel in the front parlor one day when they were doing demolition work, and they came and showed it to me." Susan says she had never seen it before and had no idea who the little girl was. The black-and-white snapshot could have been taken anywhere from the 1920s to the 50s, she suspects, and the little girl – perhaps eight years of age or so – sported a simple white dress. "I took it and put it on the mantel shelf for safe keeping, but when I went to get it the next day, it was gone. I haven't seen it to this day and I have no idea what could have happened to it."

If Susan had already harbored some misgivings that her house might be haunted by this point, the strange episode with the picture of the little girl only served to strengthen her suspicions. However, something had happened only the day before that really made her question her previously skeptical beliefs in the supernatural. The incident involved her son and the previously unseen figure of a ghostly little girl in white on the stairs. It seems that Susan had lost the old photograph of the little girl, but acquired a bona fide apparition in its place.

Her son, Susan Shearer explains, "Is not the kind of guy who

When Susan Shearer and her sister, Linda Gregory, purchased the lovely Queen Anne home at 1439 South Sixth Street, they didn't suspect the home was haunted.

tends to invent things and make them up." She says he comes across to most as a no-nonsense type of individual, the type of fellow most would consider a skeptic. "So, if he says he saw something," Shearer clarifies, "I know he must have seen something. And he says he saw the ghost of a little girl on the stairs." She had chuckled nervously and tried to shrug it off when her son had told her about an eerie encounter with a dark shadow that had mysteriously blocked the light streaming through the small square overhead where an ancient heating register had been removed for cleaning. But this time, she started to take it seriously. In remarkable detail, her son told her how he had been at the front door when the odd feeling of someone staring at him caused the hair on his arms to prickle. He turned around quickly and felt his blood turn cold as he stared at an unexpected form standing before him on the landing. A serene, disinterested gaze painted on her face, a young girl stood there and watched him, unmoving, while the rash of standing hairs spread up to the back of his neck with a shiver. A bow held her darkish hair up from her face, and she wore a plain white dress that might have served as a school dress. A second later, the vision faded and vanished.

Although she herself has never seen this little girl, Susan speculates that her appearance on the stairs holds some connection to the other strange happenings in her home and that it might have something to do with the black-and-white photo that had been found in her house. Curious to see what other secrets the house held, she dug up the deeds at the Jefferson County courthouse and pored through pages and pages of aging script.

She had discovered that the history of her home really started on July 8, 1890, when the owner of the land, Mr. W. Slaughter, had sold the land to the newly formed Victoria Land Grant Company. This real estate venture had emerged when city developers acquired the site of the former Grand Southern Exposition of 1883, dismantled the huge wooden exhibit hall that at one time covered the entire St. James Court area and then sold off plots of land in an attempt to develop Louisville's first suburb, or the *Southern Extension,* as it had been called. In July of the following year, the Victoria Land Grant Company deeded the property to Mr. John W. Gernert, and he and his family had the house until 1923, when Joseph C. Chickering bought it. He lived there with his family until 1946, at which time the Tomerlins purchased the property and called it home for the next fifty years or so.

After rummaging through the public records of the local

courthouse, she took a list of the various individuals who at one time had owned the Sixth Street property and spent an afternoon at the Louisville Free Public Library perusing the old *Caron's City Directories* in an effort to retrieve details about the home's prior inhabitants. An early precursor to today's telephone books, these useful tomes provided names and addresses of city dwellers according to street and intersection locations, as well as listed the occupations of those who resided there. Although she unearthed a trove of interesting information about the former occupants of the home, she came across nothing that might account for the ghostly apparition on the stairs. That would have to wait until I started interviewing people who used to live in the home.

Susan said she did receive some interesting information from local psychic Cheryl Glassner, however. I had put her in touch with the woman who had discovered the various "entities" that had provoked a rash of strange occurrences in Jon Huffman and Barb Cullen's house at 539 West Ormsby, and Cheryl had reportedly picked up on some very positive female energy in the Sixth Street home. "She was able to tell me a lot of things I found very useful," says Shearer, "and she also picked up on a lot of different things about my personal life, which I thought was very interesting." The most interesting information by far came when Cheryl made her way down the stairs from the second floor to the foyer at the front of the house.

A cold winter day raged, and I had met Cheryl at Susan's house to watch her do a 'reading' of the premises. She came with no prior knowledge of the house, other than the fact that strange, unexplainable incidents had been reported.

Susan had done an amazing amount of work in the several months since I had paid my first visit to the residence, and the place had a nice, cozy feel to it. The floors had a high-polished gleam to them, and I couldn't keep my eyes off of the elaborate fireplace mantels with their ornate tile inserts and built-in curio shelves. Susan had recently found a secret compartment in the mantel in the dining room and couldn't wait to show me. The place was finally shaping up, and I could tell she was happy to be home.

After she passed around steaming mugs of herbal tea and got me up to date on all her recent projects, Cheryl took out a small package and quietly unwrapped it before she started to make her way slowly around the house. "This is a pendant," she explained, "and I use it, like a pendulum, to measure the energy around us." She walked to a nearby window and held the small, dangling pendant up in the air and waited to see what would happen. Suddenly, the suspended object seemed to start swinging on its own, back and forth, and then around in long, lazy arcs. "Oh yes," replied Cheryl, "there's a lot of good energy here." For half an hour, I watched as Cheryl and Susan made their way through the house, Cheryl commenting the whole time on the antics of her pendulum while Susan listened eagerly to the reports of "strong, positive female energy" in the place. As they made their way down the front stairs, Susan sat on the steps and listened as Cheryl continued with her observations and impressions. As if suddenly distracted, the psychic stopped in mid-sentence and looked at Susan. "There's a little girl sitting next to you on the stairs, and she seems to be very happy."

For Susan Shearer, that was enough to convince her of the psychic's ability. "I think it's amazing that she picked up on all the female energy in the house," she says, "because I was getting those exact same impressions. And then when she said there was a little girl on the stairs, well, that was enough for me! I knew there had to be a reason for it all."

When I started doing research for my first book, I left notes on various online message boards and placed announcements in local newsletters informing people that I needed historical information of a ghostly nature pertaining to Old Louisville, and every once in a while someone would contact me with very useful leads. Sometimes I would receive random, unsigned postcards in the mail, kind letters, anonymous telephone messages and, more often than not, emails. This happened on a sultry evening in early summer as I polished the glasses at the table I had just set in anticipation of a dinner party I offered to host for some writer friends.

Wade Hall and Gregg Hall were the guests of honor, and since I had a break from teaching my regular load of classes, I had

*Local psychic
Cheryl Glassner uses
a pendant to detect
spirit energy.*

decided to go all out and do a proper sit-down with enough courses to impress. In the front parlor we sipped on sherry and nibbled
chicken salad canapés before seating ourselves at the table in the dining room. I popped the cork on a bottle of sparkling wine and
served the first course: fried green tomatoes with cucumber
remoulade. After that came a salad of dressed bitter greens with
grilled fennel, sweet corn and goat cheese from nearby Capriole
Farms.

   After the salad plates had been cleared, I opened a nice pinot
noir from Oregon and served broiled salmon with creamed spinach
and purple potatoes, followed by homemade lemon sorbet with
large chunks of candied ginger. We switched to a hearty Zinfandel
from northern California and then tackled the main course: roast

pork tenderloin with caper sauce, homemade egg noodles and mushroom compote. After half an hour of congenial conversation about a new play that my friend, Jerry Rodgers, had just written, we had our first dessert: rhubarb crisp with cinnamon whipped cream. (In a decadent fit of whimsy, I made a self-indulgent New Year's resolution several years ago promising that all my future dinner parties would end with *two* desserts, and since then I've lived up to my word.) After that, I passed around glasses of tawny port, and we tucked into the evening's finale, bourbon chocolate crème with butter cookies and fresh cherries.

The guests – all of them contented – had left by midnight, and I decided to check my email after cleaning a bit in the kitchen. I had only one message, and it came from a woman named Mary Barton who explained that her relatives had at one time lived at 1439 South Sixth Street. She had read my first book and wanted to know if I had heard any stories about this particular house. If not, she said, she had some stories she would be more than glad to share with me. No one, as far as I knew, other than Susan's immediate family, had any inkling about the recent strange goings-on in the lovely Queen Anne home on Sixth, and I could barely contain my eagerness as I replied to Mary's message and made arrangements to meet her the next day.

A nice breeze rustled the bright green leaves overhead the following afternoon as I approached the fountain in the middle of St. James Court. Summer hadn't quite arrived, and the oppressive humidity so typical of the warm months in Kentucky hadn't taken its stranglehold on the neighborhood yet, so the afternoon seemed unseasonably fresh. Mary hadn't showed up yet, and I walked to the railing around the fountain and leaned against it as I watched the water dance and sparkle.

An original fixture since the court's inception in the late 1800s, the Central Fountain of St. James Court marks the center of the original Southern Exposition of 1883, that precursor of today's world's fairs that put Louisville on the map and led to the development of Old Louisville as it is known today. Across from it, to the east, sits tranquil Fountain Court, its opening flanked on both sides by early examples of elegant apartment and condo buildings that caused more than one Victorian eyebrow to arch in disapproval. The swanky St. James Flats, in particular, caused quite a bit of consternation when Theophilus Conrad built it with six floors that towered over everything else on the court. Widely derided as "life on a shelf," the new-fangled apartment house offered a glimpse of city living that came across as alien to many self-respecting, upper-crust Victorians in the area. "Why would people want to live like that – stacked one on top of the other?" Society ladies would ask each other this in the gracious front parlors facing the court where they would assemble for afternoon teas. When a terrible fire destroyed the topmost floors in 1912, many old timers could hardly contain their gloating at the news that they would finally get their way and have no disproportionate structures on the court.

On the other side of the fountain, to the west, sits the former home of Madison Julius Cawein, Kentucky's first Poet Laureate. Built in 1901 in the Georgian-Revival style, it boasts a unique entry portico with columns set beneath a rounded bay to take advantage of its enviable view of the fountain. Often referred to as the "Audubon of Poetry" because of his many poems about nature, Cawein could often be seen wandering the pleasant walkways of St. James Court, stopping frequently to examine the wide variety of local flora on display there. (As coincidence would have it, the stately home recently became home to another Poet Laureate.)

Off in the distance, I could spot the turret from the Pink Palace as the leaves rustled and jostled back and forth, affording only momentary glimpses of the popular local landmark. I closed my eyes a bit and inhaled the green, leafy fragrance when my ears caught the sound of a small voice drawing near. "Hello," she said.

I opened my eyes and pivoted a bit. Mary Barton, a smallish woman with graying hair pulled up in the back, stood before me. We made our introductions and exchanged a bit of polite small talk before she suggested that we start strolling around St. James Court as she told me her story.

Mary Barton, a native of southern California, had come to Louisville in the 1940s when her husband decided to move back to the area to take care of an ailing mother and father. "My husband, John, was born in Bardstown, but his parents moved to Louisville when he was ten," she explained. "His mother's side of the family has roots that go all the way back to Daniel Boone and some other early pioneer names that settled the state. They were always really proud of that."

Within two years of their arrival in Louisville, said Mary, both her mother-in-law and father-in-law had died, as had been anticipated, and she and her young husband were free to enjoy their newfound freedom. "We lived with his parents on Zane Street," she commented, "and after they passed on, we inherited the house from them." The house, still standing today, counted as one of the more modest examples of residential architecture in the neighborhood, but Mary claims the staid brick structure felt "like a real mansion" to them once she and her husband had it all to themselves. "It was a large home with three floors, and we lived there for almost five years, and had a great time," she says. "The house was really close to downtown, and some of our happiest memories came from there."

We strolled past the intricate limestone façade of the enormous Conrad-Caldwell House with all its Richardsonian Romanesque detail at the mouth of St. James Court and then past the whimsical Moorish arches of the Venetian Gothic masterpiece at 1412 where local pottery legend Mary Alice Hadley had her original studio. As we walked, Mary Barton regaled me with interesting stories of life in Louisville in the 1950s, a time when the area hadn't quite reached the apex of its decline. According to Mary, the Old Louisville neighborhood still occupied a place of honor among the city's various neighborhoods back then, and twice as many elegant mansions dotted the entire district. "It was a place with a very vibrant society life," she recalls, "and tradition was alive and well. Huge Victorian mansions were on the way out as people moved to the suburbs, but this was still a classy part of town."

At the southern end of St. James Court, we turned right on Belgravia Court and made our way down the narrow sidewalks while the constant flames in the gas lamps flickered and added a bit of needless illumination and romance to our stroll. At the Sixth

Street exit, we turned right again and steered our way north towards Central Park, and when we came to an unexpected stop in front of the tidy little house at 1439, I had all but forgotten the reason I had arranged to meet Mrs. Barton in the first place.

Without looking at me, Mary raised her hand and pointed at the wooden structure with its neat colors of blue and beige. "I have seen some *very* strange things in that house," she stated matter-of-factly, "things that I will never forget." When I coaxed her for more information she told me the story of the little girl in white on the front stairs.

"I'm kin to the Chickerings," she said, "and they used to own this house." My ears immediately perked up at the recognition of that last name. "When we lived in the house over on Zane Street, I'd spend a lot of time over here visiting my Aunt Viola. Taking care of two elderly people was hard," she recalls, "and it was nice to get out of the house whenever I could." But it seems that these visits weren't always pleasant, either.

"Aunt Viola's husband – Joe, or Uncle Chick as we used to call him – had a hard time of it the older he got, and towards the end of his life he suffered from dementia. My aunt had a horrible time taking care of him, and it really wore her out." When she realized she hadn't made any mention of the ghostly phenomena in the house that she had alluded to, Mary looked at me and said, "He always talked about the little girl in white who used to come and talk to him. But there was no little girl in white who lived there. We all thought he was just out of his mind and ignored it. There were always different ghosts floating around the neighborhood, like the one over at the corner of Twelfth and Zane Streets, but I never took those things too seriously."

That is, until Mary witnessed an apparition herself one day.

"Back then nobody locked their doors – there was no need to – and I had just stopped by for a visit," she remembers. "I opened the door and walked inside and called out for my aunt, and I had just started to head down the hallway to the kitchen at the back of the house, when this strange sensation came over me." Mary says she stopped dead in her tracks and remained motionless while the hairs on her arms stood on end and sent shivers running down her neck and back. "It was almost like I was paralyzed," she explains. "I couldn't move a muscle, just like in one of them dreams where you're scared and try to scream out and can't do anything at all."

Out of the corner of her eye, but well within her line of vision, she perceived something to the left, where the stairs went up to the next floor. "I moved my eyes to the left a bit," she says, "and then I saw her! A little girl in a white dress as plain as day. Standing on the stairs looking right at me!" Mary says the vision appeared to look right through her and had a translucent quality about it. "She just stood there and stared, but she wasn't looking at me – just *through* me. And, the funny thing is – I could see right through her, too." Transfixed, Mary remembers counting the steps she could see on the other side of the ghostly denizen on the staircase. "She was all shimmery-like, and I counted eight steps behind her before she vanished and was gone!" The front door then swung open and closed with a violent slam.

At that moment, Mary's aunt emerged from the kitchen and told the stunned woman to join her at the table for a cup of coffee, admonishing her for slamming the door in the process. "I was visibly shaken when I sat down," Mary says, "and the first thing my aunt says is 'Good grief, you look like you just saw a ghost!' Then she narrowed her eyes at me and asked if I had seen something in her house." By the time Mary replied that she had, her aunt had already guessed as much, and confessed that she had also seen the strange apparition. "We realized that Uncle Chick might not have been so crazy after all!"

Mary Barton claims she saw the strange vision – always on the front steps – several more times during the next year or so. And she says other strange things happened in her aunt's home on South Sixth Street. "The doors and windows used to open and close by themselves," she recalls, "and on one occasion, I even saw a large skillet fly through the air and land in the sink with a terrible ruckus. It got to be that I got nervous whenever I had to go over there." It wasn't till later that Mary's Aunt Viola told her the reason for the haunting.

"At first she denied that there could be ghosts in her house," recalls Mary, "and whenever I pressed her for more information about the house, she always skirted the issue. One day, though, I just kept after her, and she finally broke down and told me about the accident."

According to her aunt, the Chickerings had at one time had boarders in their house, two of which were a young, single mother and her eight-year-old daughter. "I guess they were hard up and needed cash," Mary speculates. "And this would have been during the Depression years, so it would stand to reason. Lots of people in the area had to take in boarders to make ends meet." It appears that the young girl had some behavioral problems, and her mother sometimes had a hard time keeping the young girl from running out the front door and into the street. One night, just as dusk was falling, the young girl ran down the front stairs and out the door as her mother washed up for the evening meal. "The mother wasn't quick enough, and the next thing people heard," says Mary Barton, "was a honking and the terrible screech of brakes. They all ran outside and found that the young girl had been hit and killed by a passing motorist." She had been wearing a simple, white dress. Not too long thereafter, Uncle Chick began complaining about the apparition of the little girl on the steps at the front of the house at 1439 South Sixth Street.

Had he really seen the ghostly apparition of the young girl who had lived in the house, or did this merely signal the onslaught of dementia? Mary Barton has convinced herself that her uncle had seen the same strange manifestation that she herself had witnessed, and for her, it was enough to learn that a little girl had been tragically run down and killed in front of the house so many years ago. Her aunt and uncle eventually moved from the house on South Sixth Street, and Mary Barton says she had never returned to the charming Queen Anne house until the day she and I had strolled around the neighborhood. When I told her that current occupants had indeed reported strange sightings of a young girl in white in the very same location she had mentioned, she smiled slightly and suggested that we resume our stroll through the neighborhood.

ABOUT THE CORNER OF
TWELFTH AND ZANE

For many years, inhabitants of Old Louisville and the adjacent neighborhoods have talked about a mysterious apparition that shows itself on occasion at the corner of Twelfth and Zane, an area that lies outside of the historic preservation district and to the west of the rail lines that run parallel to Ninth Street. Although nothing much of the original neighborhood that occupied "the other side of the tracks" remains, this was a vibrant neighborhood where many railroad employees and warehouse workers took up residence in the modest shotgun cottages and brick and frame homes. Long before Old Louisville had established itself as a bastion for the wealthy and an enclave for the elite, this area – the Limerick district – had emerged as a gritty immigrant neighborhood with its own supply of notoriety, phantoms and dirty secrets. One of these phantoms, it would appear, still haunts the area she called home in life, and it seems she has a score to settle.

"It scared the life out of me!" reports Jon Walsh, a Limerick native who has sighted the strange apparition on more than one occasion. "When I was a kid, we always used to talk about the 'dead woman' on the corner, but I never dreamed I'd actually see it in person one day." Although the site offers little more than gravel surface parking and industrial-looking warehouses today, rumor has it that an unfortunate woman once met her untimely end in a house that stood there, and her sad – and frustrated – ghost still inhabits the spot. "My grandparents always used to talk about her, warn us about her," explains Walsh, "and they said she had been killed by her own husband many years before and that she was still very angry about it. I guess I would be, too," he readily concedes.

"The first time I saw her would have been sometime in the late 70s, I reckon," he says. "It was summer time, and we were out riding our bikes along the railroad tracks. It had just started to get dark out, and we found ourselves approaching the corner of Twelfth and Zane. All the others in the group were speeding on ahead of me, and I was the very last one. I turned my head and saw this strange

Although the house that occupied the site no longer stands, local legend has it that the lost spirit of a battered wife from the 1870s still lingers on.

form standing there near the corner where the street sign is. At first I thought it was someone out taking a walk, but then I noticed that she had on really old clothes with blood stains on them. Then I noticed that she was really glaring at me, like I did something wrong, so I got out of there as fast as I could." A second later, when he looked over his shoulder, he saw that she had disappeared.

"The next time I saw her was a few years after that," Walsh remembers. "It was evening, and I was driving by in my car and saw the exact same thing – a woman in old-fashioned clothes, dirty with blood stains – but she didn't seem as angry as the time before; in fact, she almost seemed sad. I actually felt sorry for her. I wasn't quite as spooked as when I saw her the first time, so I paid better attention. I could tell she wasn't real. She looked like she was float-ing and she seemed almost see-through to me, and her reflection – or whatever it was – looked shiny." According to the man, she lin-gered a second or two and then began to fade away.

Others besides Jon Walsh have reported the same vision, and it seems that several overriding similarities characterize most sightings of the phantom near the corner of Twelfth and Zane. Aside from her bloodstained garments, most report an overwhelming sense of sadness, anger and foreboding. "She was resentful about something alright," remarks Tom Street, a warehouse worker who had an unsettling encounter with the unblithe spirit one night as he unloaded freight from the back of a semi truck parked near the corner of Twelfth and Zane. "I looked up as I carried a bunch of boxes up the ramp, and I saw this cloudy thing standing out by the corner. At first I thought I was imagining things, but I blinked my eyes a couple of times and realized there was something there. I stared, and I could see a woman staring right back at me. I could feel that she wasn't happy; she was very sad. I saw what I think were stains on her dress. Maybe *blood?* I don't know. Before I had a chance to decide, she was gone. I never saw her again, a fact that I'm not too depressed about."

In his interesting book *Murder in Old Kentucky,* Richmond author Keven McQueen reports on a tragic case of domestic abuse from 1878 in Louisville that more than likely explains the source for the eerie haint at the corner of Twelfth and Zane. On April 18, "an inebriated [Robert] Anderson returned to his home at the corner of Twelfth and Zane Street, Louisville, in his usual bad temper. His wife [Margaret] had been washing clothes for money all day and was in no mood to endure his abuse. He demanded that she turn over her wages so he could buy more drinks. She told him that she was going to leave him. Anderson retorted by reaching for his knife."

Although it would appear that Robert, an engineer at a local stoneworks, earned a decent wage, McQueen reports that he evidently drank away his paycheck and left his wife and five children lacking for food and basic necessities on a daily basis. Not content with this abuse alone, the worthless lout had also threatened or attempted to kill his wife on no less than three separate occasions. It came as little surprise, then, when Anderson actually attacked his wife on April 18, leaving her "on the floor and bleeding from wounds in the chest and neck." Although she managed to get free of the lunatic and received timely first aid from neighbors, the long-suffering woman succumbed to her injuries nine days later. Police arrested Robert Anderson, and he died at the gallows almost two years later, but only after a sensational trial in which his lawyers attempted – *of all things!* – to argue the defendant's sanity and to impugn his wife's character.

On an interesting side note, the presiding judge in the case had honored Anderson's final wish and granted him something unheard of in Kentucky prior to that: a *private* execution in the jail yard. A rather dignified death by 19th-century standards, it offered a departure – somewhat undeserved, perhaps – devoid both of public humiliation and bloodthirsty onlookers.

Is the apparition that has been sighted at the corner of Twelfth and Zane Streets that of the unfortunate Margaret Anderson? Is her ghost angry because her husband never received the full extent of the punishment meted out to him? Or is this earthbound spirit simply enraged that she could have prevented her own death? As is all too often the case in purported instances of domestic violence, Mrs. Anderson had talked police officers out of arresting her wife-beating husband during previous disturbances. This unfortunate decision might have cost the poor woman her life in the end, her unsound reasoning the final nail in a coffin hammered together by years of spousal abuse and alcohol-fueled violence.

But . . . ghosts are restless creatures by nature, and it takes more than wood and nails to restrain them. Spirits that have found no rest know no boundaries, and only peace can put them at ease, can smooth their paths to tranquility. If these airy wraiths haven't calmed their rage or haven't realized a transition from one realm to the next, the cooling, black winds of providence carry them aloft and condemn them to languish on where they last knew calm, be it a house that no longer stands or a lonely street corner that hints at a bygone era.

Chapter 4

THE PINK PALACE

ajestically rising from the middle of Belgravia Court and towering over the south end of St. James Court, the Pink Palace boasts a history as colorful and storied as any of the hundreds of grand mansions that dot the Old Louisville historic district. Its most striking feature, a spire-like turret at its western end, hints at the Chateauesque design that guided its construction in 1891, a year that saw the addition of many elegant residences to the burgeoning St. James Court neighborhood. Word had spread that Louisville's ultra sophisticates would be calling the newly developed suburb home, and, by the turn of the next century, land in the city's trendiest neighborhood commanded premium prices that only the wealthiest could afford. St. James Court – with its would-be aristocrats and devoted Anglophiles – had become a neighborhood of movers and shakers. Bankers lived next door to well-to-do merchants, distillers and tobacco barons, and newspapermen resided amongst local business magnates and city dignitaries. A smattering of well-known writers, artists and poets added a bit of respected sophistication to the mix. These men of

Known as the Pink Palace for years, the lovely château-style residence at the south end of St. James Court reportedly harbors a friendly ghost.

influence would need a place to congregate, and this place would be the Pink Palace.

Although people in the area have called this magnificent home the "Pink Palace" for ages, it originally began its life on St. James Court as the "Casino." Long before Las Vegas and Monte Carlo branded this innocent Italian word for a small country home with its current gambling connotation, *casinos* served as relaxing country getaways where the affluent could unwind and pursue those pastimes typically pursued by the affluent. In Victorian England and America, prestigious neighborhoods had their own casinos where families could meet for day outings and wind down as much as allowed by rigid societal norms. In Victorian Kentucky, well-to-do residents of its largest city added their own twist to the local casino, and it became a haven for an exclusively male clientele. Also known as the Gentlemen's Club of St. James Court, it served as a crony-rid-

Jeff Perry and Kent Thompson reside in the former St. James Court Gentlemen's Club and Casino, one of the most storied structures in all of Old Louisville. The 1890s mansion retains all of its original woodwork and stunning Victorian detail.

One of Old Louisville's crown jewels, the lovely Pink Palace has rooms that hint at the elegance of a bygone era - and a phantom gentleman known as Avery.

den escape where local bigwigs could sit at ease while enjoying bourbon and cigars, diverting themselves with an occasional hand of poker and plenty of neighborhood gossip.

The surroundings – of course – seemed comfortable and luxurious without being ostentatious. A spacious foyer invited gentlemen inside, where an attendant usually stood at the ready in case members needed to dispose of their coats and hats. Enveloped in the warm glow of polished parquet floors and oaken trimmings, a grand staircase framed with double arches and gleaming columns twisted its way to the upper floors where gentlemen could conduct their business. On either side of the entry hall, plush chairs, comfortable divans and card tables completed the two main clubrooms where waiters in starched collars served drinks and provided the most recent copies of the various city newspapers. During the day, sunlight filtered its way through the impressive art glass windows encased in the stairwell and littered the lobby with random jewels of multicolored light. During the evening, after long shadows made their way down the brick sidewalks and faded into darkness, the gas lanterns clicked on with a hiss and bathed the stylish interior with a warm glow that highlighted the burgundy draperies and embossed wall coverings. Tucked away in the contented confines of their respectable dwellings, most of the residents of St. James Court pulled their curtains to and politely ignored the palatial structure that dominated the south end of the court. It seems that – by night – the Gentlemen's Club of St. James Court took on another life, one that catered to the more carnal nature of its members.

At least that's what Kent Thompson and Jeff Perry, the current owners of the Pink Palace, told me one evening as we sat around the dining table at my house and listened to stories about their intriguing home while icy winter winds roared outside. In front of the fire in the front parlor, we had sipped cups of mulled cider spiked with bourbon as I passed around a silver tray with Shaker cheese wafers and smoked spoonfish from Shuckman's. At the table, we had just begun the dinner with bowls of squash bisque and glasses of a nice, fruity white Riesling from Equus Run Vineyards in nearby Midway, when Kent alluded to this seedier side of the Pink Palace. "The upstairs rooms have closets that are *exceptionally* large," he commented, "and this was always a bit puzzling, because many homes back in the late 1800s didn't have a lot of closets. It seems that early tax assessors considered closets actual rooms in a home and charged the property owners accordingly." We switched to a Vidal blanc from the same vineyard for the next course – broiled salmon with beurre rouge and julienne pickle and mashed new red potatoes – and Jeff couldn't resist interjecting, "It turns our that their female counterparts *conducted their business* in these little rooms!"

I opened a nice cabernet sauvignon from Napa Valley, and we all enjoyed it with the next two courses (coq au vin with homemade spätzle and pearl onions, and beef tenderloin with mushroom ragout, scalloped corn and asparagus vinaigrette), while Kent and Jeff finished the interesting yarn about how their house acquired the nickname of the Pink Palace. By the time I served various cheeses with sweetmilk rolls and homemade applesauce and then chocolate gingerbread and thick cream flavored with nutmeg and Galliano for dessert, we had all become quite familiar with the history of the building known as the Pink Palace.

It seems that the storied past of the Gentlemen's Club of St. James Court would be a short-lived one, and not too long after it opened its doors to the wealthy male residents of the neighborhood, it passed to a local family who called it home until 1910. By an ironic turn of fate, the next tenant to occupy the lovely, red-brick structure at 1473 St. James Court would be none other than the local chapter of the WCTU, that largest of all women's organizations in the Gilded Age known as the Women's Christian Temperance Union. Although the organization founded in 1874 still exists today and can claim many admirable achievements in the areas of voting rights for women and labor law, most people today remember it today for its spirited campaigns against the consumption of alcohol, not to mention their unfavorable views on tobacco, gambling and prostitution. Many doubt that the Volstead Act of 1919 would have passed without their well organized 'pray-ins' at local saloons and their fierce abstinence rallies across the nation, events that ushered in the bleak period from 1920 to 1933 known as Prohibition.

At least many "thirsty" citizens considered it a bleak period; teetotalers considered it a triumph for their enlightened ideals, and the aristocrats of the Kentucky prohibitionist movement now had a palace in which to gloat. The first thing the Women's Christian Temperance Union did was to paint the former gentlemen's club pink as a means of touting their feminist leanings and, moreover, to distance themselves from the building's sordid past. The dazzling shade of pink would illuminate the path for wayward drinkers in the neighborhood, and it remained long after the WCTU vacated the premises and after Congress finally repealed the Volstead Act, much to the delight of many Depression-weary Americans in search of a good – and legal – drink.

Considering the *colorful* past of the Pink Palace, would anyone be surprised to learn that at least one spirit lingers on in the comfortable home at the southern end of the expansive urban green known as St. James Court? Although the current owners have yet to see the resident ghost they acquired with their purchase of the former casino and gentlemen's club, previous owners have had unsettling encounters with him, and they say his name is *Avery.* Although he has heard mostly positive things about Avery, current owner Jeff Perry hasn't yet decided that he needs to verify the existence of his ghost. "I don't want a ghost in my house!" he exclaims. "I'm afraid if I talk about him too much, he'll show up and won't go away!"

Jeff's reservations aside, it seems that most residents of the Pink Palace have appreciated this ghostly presence, whose appearance has been attributed to that of a *crisis apparition.* Parapsychological experts claim that these types of manifestations usually take place when an individual finds him or herself in imminent danger and sends the body's spirit on as a type of emissary to warn loved ones of the crisis or to prepare them for news of the individual's passing. Some also claim that crisis apparitions can occur when ghosts sense danger and make an appearance so as to warn certain individuals of possible harm. People who have experienced Avery at the Pink Palace suggest that his sightings involve the latter, because he usually makes an appearance when something bad threatens to happen.

Strange experiences with Avery in the former gentlemen's club have convinced Jenny Dickerson that the ghostly sightings involve a friendly spirit, a sort of harbinger or portend, if you will, who still lingers on in the splendid environs as a way of watching out and protecting those who inhabit his home. Decades ago, Dickerson sublet a basement apartment in the Pink Palace when she did her graduate work in library science at nearby University of Louisville, and she claims to be the person who "discovered" and named Avery. If truth in fact has any bearing on the curious incidents that transpired during her residency, it would appear that Avery, indeed, has stayed on at the Pink Palace to guard the place from danger.

"Back in the 60s and 70s when I was studying at U of L," she explains, "I rented out an apartment in the cellar of the old casino. And if anyone had told me back then that I would see a ghost one day, I would have said they were crazy – because I never believed in ghosts and such . . . that is, until I saw one myself one day. I don't care if people believe me or not! It happened, and I know it happened, even though I cannot explain why such things happen. People can take it or leave it, but I always tell my story to those interested in hearing it."

Jenny's story began one evening as she stood at a counter in the kitchen chopping vegetables for a soup she had just put on the stove. As if to foreshadow the appearance of the strange vision, a fierce wind roared outside and caused the kitchen windows to rattle in their casements. When the soup started to boil and fill the small space with an inviting aroma, Jenny tossed in the chopped vegetables and turned around to deposit the cutting board in the sink.

"I froze," she says. "There, standing right in front of me, in the doorway that led to the bathroom, was a man! He wasn't real, though, because I could see right through him. He was relatively tall – about 6 feet, I'd say – and he was wearing an old-fashioned duck suit, sort of like the one Colonel Sanders always wore. And like Mr. Sanders, he had on a black string tie. His hair was white, too, but his face didn't look like the Colonel's at all. He was clean shaven and very aristocratic-looking, and he had an incredible mane of wavy hair. It was white, I think, but it could have been any color, I guess, because the way the thing presented itself, it was all in black and white.

"I just stared at it and didn't know what to do. I wasn't really afraid, but I still couldn't believe what was happening. I thought I was imagining the whole thing for sure and I rubbed my eyes a couple of times, and he was still there, just looking at me, no expression on his face at all. I'm not even sure if he could see me, because his face didn't register any emotion. It was so odd. Then, all of a sudden, he was gone!

"Well, my heart was racing a hundred miles a minute, so I sat down at the kitchen table and tried to figure out what I had just seen. I wasn't tired; I wasn't under stress or anything, so I'm sure I saw something real. I concluded, therefore, that I had seen a ghost, which, of course, seemed the most logical explanation under the circumstance. It was quite an earth-shattering moment for me, because I had never believed in that kind of thing, and now I had seen one for myself, and *had* to believe. I'll never forget that first vision as long as I live!

"The curious thing is that when I regained my composure and got back to my soup, I jokingly wondered to myself if I'd have any run-ins with 'Avery' again. I decided he wasn't there to harm me, so it really didn't bother me one way or the other. But I stopped for a minute. Why did I call him 'Avery?' I realized that nobody had told me his name. It just came out of the blue that his name was Avery. I guess I sort of sensed it, that's all, but after that, everyone always called him 'Avery.'

"Well, I did have another encounter with Avery. It happened to be that very same night! I put the soup on simmer and ran some hot water for a bath. I put in some bubbles and got in so I could soak for half an hour or so. It was nice, and I just sat there and unwound and relaxed in the warm, soapy water. I had just started to doze off when I had a strange sensation – sort of like someone was staring at me. I opened my eyes, and there he was again!

"He was standing in the doorway to the bathroom again, just staring at me, no expression on his face, nothing. Wearing the same clothes and all. Like before, he didn't scare me or anything, but for some reason, I was afraid all of a sudden. Not of him, but of *something*. I panicked a bit and looked around the bathroom, and when I directed my eyes back to the doorway, Avery had vanished into thin air. He was gone, but I still had the same uneasy feeling, so I jumped up and out of the tub, and grabbed a towel and my bathrobe and ran through the doorway.

"No sooner had I exited the bathroom than I heard a terrible crash of breaking glass and splashing water. I turned around, and there was water all over the place and one of the windows was broken out. I was filled with a terrible dread and had no idea what had just happened, so I picked up the phone and called the police. They were there a minute later, and then we were able to figure out what had happened.

"Two burglars were trying to break into my apartment – that's what happened. They had taken a big cement block and threw it through the window that was right *above* the bathtub. It landed right in the tub – right where my head would have been – and smashed the whole thing to bits. It would have killed me, without a doubt. I guess the crooks got scared when they heard the police coming and decided against coming inside. If Avery hadn't warned me, I would have stayed in the bathtub, and who knows what awful things would have happened that night? I'm convinced he showed up to let me know I was in danger. He saved my life."

Jenny Dickerson says she finished her degree the next year and moved out to the West Coast when she got a prestigious job at a university library. Although she never had any subsequent visits from Avery, she kept in touch with people who lived in the Pink Palace, and it didn't surprise her to learn that various residents had encountered the aristocratic southern gentleman with wavy hair in the linen suit with the black string tie. "I talked to my friends who lived there," says Dickerson, "and they said he appeared to them one night in the kitchen. The next minute, a smoke alarm went off in the utility room because a small fire had started due to faulty wiring. They put it out right away, but said it would have been a disaster if Avery hadn't showed up." True to form, he only made appearances when danger threatened the occupants of 1473 St. James Court.

"The really funny thing about the story is something interesting I discovered years later, after I moved back to Louisville to teach at the schools here," Jenny explains. "It was at least twenty years later, and I found myself back in Louisville. I had pretty much forgotten about Avery and the Pink Palace, because I lived in another part of town and didn't get down to Old Louisville much.

"I was helping a friend with a grant proposal that required me to do some research at the Louisville Free Public Library. It's a beautiful old building from the early 1900s, and I always love going there to do research. Well, anyway, one day I was down there, digging through some old newspaper clippings, and the topic of investigation was totally unrelated to Old Louisville or the Pink Palace. I had pretty much found what I needed and was getting ready to leave, but as I put the clippings back in their box, I noticed one of them that I hadn't read because it had a familiar picture on it. It was a picture of 1473 St. James Court.

"I decided to read the article, and it turned out to be a story about the old gentlemen's club and casino and how it was going out of business. They gave some descriptions of the interior and all the wonderful old furniture inside, and told how a family had recently acquired it and were planning on living there. It was very interesting, but the big shock came when I got to the end of the article, because there, at the bottom of the page, was a small black and white photo of a distinctive-looking gentleman with a white suit, black string tie, and wild, wavy hair. The caption underneath said something to the effect that 'Mr. *Avery* and his family have recently acquired the former casino and gentlemen's club and will be calling it home.' I was absolutely dumbfounded! There was an actual Avery, and his picture matched the apparition I had seen to a tee!"

Although I have been unable to locate the newspaper article Dickerson claims to have seen some twenty years ago, I did manage to locate all the deeds for the property at 1473 St. James Court, and Mr. Avery was indeed the first man to call the old casino and gentlemen's club home. A wealthy merchant and manufacturer of farm equipment and machinery, he cut a dignified figure on the court and had the reputation of being a typical Kentucky Colonel.

Avery, it seems, counted as just one of many colorful tenants that called the colorful Pink Palace home. Another early resident, Dr. George H. Wilson – or Dr. "Eardrum" Wilson, as he was known – made a name and fortune for himself after inventing the Wilson Eardrum in 1913, a dubious precursor to today's hearing aides, and he reportedly owned the first automobile to motor its way around St. James Court. In the 1990s, a reportedly cantankerous artist took up residence in the old casino and became embroiled in somewhat of a local scandal when he threatened to change the color scheme of the lovely Pink Palace. After numerous battles and stop-work orders from the Louisville Landmarks Commission, a compromise was reached and the characteristic pink color was retained, albeit in a rather more bedazzling shade of pink and with the addition of lavender trim that has caused more than a few eyebrows to arch in bewilderment. It seems that Kent Thompson and Jeff Perry have big shoes to fill in assuming custodianship of one of the most storied – and *colorful* – homes on the court, but I'm sure they will manage nicely, and I wish them all the luck in the world.

ABOUT THE LOUISVILLE
FREE PUBLIC LIBRARY

It seems that whenever aging stacks of musty books and stately old buildings of brick and stone come together, phantoms of the past invariably spring to life and jump from the very pages that have ensnared their stories for posterity, their haunted recollections imbuing the hallowed spaces with both a sense of permanence and wistful nostalgia. As a result, stories of haunted libraries abound in the United States, and more than one of them can be found in the Bluegrass State, where early settlers and city fathers held books and reading in very high esteem. Located between Old Louisville and the downtown area, the Louisville Free Public Library has apparently been a favorite haunt for more than just bookworms and biblio-philes during its century of existence; word has it that a ghostly librarian still roams the hallways of the jewel of Louisville's city library system, and it seems that she still has a job to do.

The second of nine Carnegie libraries built in Jefferson County in the early 1900s, the Louisville Free Public Library came into existence in 1906 after a national competition sifted through designs from prominent firms from across the country and finally chose the classic Beaux Arts plans of Louisville architect George Tachau. Taking Andrew Carnegie up on his offer to pay for libraries if cities assumed responsibility for their maintenance and upkeep, local planners collaborated with Tachau and his partner, Lewis F. Pilcher, to establish what would become the *Main Branch*. According to the *Louisville Guide* by Gregory A. Luhan, Dennis Domer and David Mohney, "the library adapts classical motifs in particular through the clustered and fluted Ionic columns and orna-mental friezes. The project is well-crafted with mosaics, paintings, a stained-glass barrel vault, and white marble floors and trim on the interior. The entrance is constructed of a set of large bronze doors at the center of the columned portico on the south façade." A weath-er-beaten statue of "Know-Nothing" George Prentice that used to occupy a prominent position over the entrance to the old *Courier-Journal* building sits in front of this majestic portico. On the western side of the building towers a large bronze of Abraham Lincoln, his serene gaze taking in the traffic that makes its way up and down Fourth Street. On the inside, a vague, misty form – oddly reminiscent of the stereotypical schoolmarms that populated American libraries in the early 1900s – has been said to hover effortlessly between the stacks, her figure translucent and bright as she floats a good foot or two off the ground.

"She looked just like one of them librarians you'd see in an old movie," clarifies Sam Loftus, a former employee of the main branch building at 301 York Street. "It was night time, around 9:00 in the evening in the summer, and we were just getting ready to close up. I went walking through the stacks, to make sure no one was left inside, and I had just turned the corner in the nonfiction section when I saw her." Loftus claims he encountered a mysterious apparition with an armload of books who appeared to reshelf them as he stared on in disbelief. "It was like she was two feet off the ground!" he recalls, "and she was just going about her business of putting the books back in place. She had on round spectacles and her hair was up in a bun, and she wore a high-waisted, long skirt and a long-sleeved blouse. I tell you, it was just how you'd expect a librarian to look fifty or a hundred years ago."

Loftus speculates he stood and observed the strange sight for twenty or thirty seconds before the ghostly librarian looked up and saw him standing there. "And she saw me; I know she did," he says, "because I could see it in her eyes, the recognition, except she looked like she was a little perplexed or something. She just floated there in midair for another second or two, and then she slowly started to fade away, and then she was gone." Thoroughly unnerved, Loftus returned to his post and clocked out, not bothering to check the rest of the building. "I didn't care if anyone was left inside," he says. "All I know is I just wanted to get out of there. I had heard stories of books flying out of the shelves all by themselves, and that a mysterious vision of a woman took place every now and then, but I never believed it, *till that night.*"

Although other people – patrons of the library included – have reported similar sightings, nobody has any concrete explana-

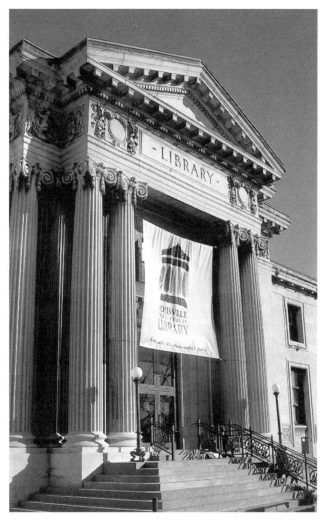

Vague forms and shadowy apparitions have been reported after hours in the Louisville Free Public Library.

tions that could account for this strange yet comforting apparition that lurks in the Louisville Free Public Library. Perfunctory research has yielded no clues, either, and no record has been made of a former librarian with reason to linger on at her former place of employ. Long-time employees of the library have reported never seeing any such visions, and many remain skeptical as to the existence of ghosts and otherworldly creatures. Many doubt that spirits even haunt the library in the first place since the area where most sightings have occurred happens to be in a newer addition from the 1960s.

Nonetheless, others have reported the same spectral vision – that of a long-skirted woman with a white blouse and glasses in the elegant lobby of the 1906 structure. She has been known to hover wordlessly over the intricate mosaics of the floor with her load of books, at times oblivious of those around her as she skims the surface of the present and darts in and out of the past. Beneath the sedate and sober gazes of the faded murals overhead, she goes on with her business of books and bindings, her own story consigned – for the time being – to the unwritten pages of history.

Chapter 5

1464 ST. JAMES COURT

Perhaps more than any other location in Old Louisville, St. James Court – along with its adjoining walking court, Belgravia Court – has managed to preserve a perfect slice of the past. Although trees have sprouted up and toppled, paint has chipped and faded, mortar has crumbled and blown away in the autumn winds, the original and *true* sense of the neighborhood persists here, offering a glimpse of unadulterated Americana that hasn't been disfigured by brutal wrecking balls or thoughtless developers. Although a century counts as little more than a blip on the timeline of humanity, it offers more than enough time for legends to take root and send up leafy canopies that shade the truth with dappled sunlight and sparkle. Fact becomes fiction, and fiction becomes reality in places like Old Louisville, and only sticklers for detail complain when a good story can't be proven.

One endearing story from the neighborhood involves the lovely stone house at 1464 St. James Court. Said to be the second home built on the court, it has played host to more than a century's worth of families, hardship and sorrow. Although prior generations have moved on, it seems ghostly phenomena remain behind to remind current inhabitants about the phantoms of the past that still call Old Louisville home. In this case no specters have materialized out of thin air and then vanished; no invisible hands have caused a person's hair to rise in fright; no cold spots have put a chill on the evening's festivities and no flickering lights have cast momentary doubt on the host's good intentions. In this case, all that remains is a sound, and a solitary one at that, that hints at a tragedy in the past, a tragedy that has left its audible mark on the present. Those who have experienced the phantom noise report that it usually occurs in the evening around 7:00, and it seems to resonate from the foyer area at the front of the house. A single pistol or revolver shot is all they hear, and no amount of coaxing can convince them that it might be a noise coming from the street or somewhere else outside.

For years, people have talked about the "ghostly gunshot" that still echoes through the halls of 1464 St. James Court. Although the current owners, new arrivals Doug and Karen Keller, have yet to experience this unexplained phenomena for themselves, they have become well-acquainted with the story. It seems that their spacious home at the southern end of the green boulevard known as St. James Court one time bore witness to a terrible accident. Time may have blurred some of the details associated with the story, but most people have still heard the same tale.

World War II had just ended, and the youngest son of the family who inhabited 1464 St. James Court had just returned from battle in Europe. He had left a sweetheart behind in Louisville, so the first thing he did when arriving back in town was to prepare for their marriage. He sent her flowers, he took her out dancing and for dinners at elegant restaurants, and one night in spring, he proposed to her – on bended knee – while she sat on a bench in nearby Central Park. She accepted his offer, and the two made plans to announce their engagement. The romance held special poignancy since the young soldier had sustained life-threatening injuries in battle during his last month of service that almost prevented him from returning to his betrothed in the first place.

A month after his arrival in Louisville, the boy's family threw

Decades after a tragic accident, a phantom gunshot supposedly still rings out in the foyer of Doug and Karen Keller's home at 1464 St. James Court.

a wonderful engagement party at their comfortable home. A lavish buffet had been laid out, and friends and relatives from the neighborhood sipped cocktails and danced to the music of a local orchestra that had been hired for the event. As the evening reached a climax, the groom-to-be's father – bottle of champagne in hand – stopped the orchestra and mounted the stairs in the foyer. Corks popped and flew through the air, and – after a touching speech by the father – all present toasted the young couple and made the engagement official. The music resumed, congratulations were rendered, and it appeared that the fiancés had embarked upon a new stage of their lives together without a hitch. But, Fate – that worst of all party crashers – would evidently deal them a different hand, one that didn't include a life together.

The story has it that several of the young man's army buddies showed up to pay their respects shortly before 7:00, and talk soon turned from girls to guns. The young man, it seems, had recently acquired a new revolver and he decided to fetch it from its location inside a drawer in a table in the foyer so his Marine friends could admire it. The music danced. Spirits soared. But the Fates had already begun to undo the threads of his would-be life of wedded bliss by the time his hand reached down, pulled the drawer open and extracted the firearm. In a tragic fluke, the gun misfired in his hand and sent an errant bullet flying through the air. The unintended victim happened to be the young and lovely bride-to-be who stood only yards away.

She died on the spot, and the much-celebrated wedding never took place. The phantom gunshot supposedly still rings out on occasion in the same foyer where the young couple enjoyed an enticing glimpse of happiness – be it ever so fleeting – so many years ago. Echoing like a voice from the past, it is a sad reminder of sorrow and tragedy that refuses to fade away.

Memories, on the other hand, do fade away and become less reliable with age, and no one in the neighborhood claims to have firsthand knowledge of this sad accident. Countless individuals – of course – assert that they know of a distant relative, or a friend of a friend, who happened to be present for the ordeal, but when it comes down to facts and eyewitness accounts of the fatal mishap, there is very little concrete evidence to substantiate this story.

The most convincing bit of information that this legend might indeed have a basis in fact came one September afternoon as I stood in the kitchen and prepared dinner for my Thursday night group of friends. I had just marinated a batch of large, freshwater prawns in bourbon and lemon juice and had tossed them on the grill when I got a call from a Third Street neighbor, JoAnn Calentano, who also happens to be a great source of information in the area. JoAnn has also been very generous in providing me leads for various stories about hauntings in Old Louisville, and this day she had an intriguing story to share.

JoAnn had been visiting with Deb Riall of the Conrad-Caldwell House, and the two had been catching up on interesting stories in the neighborhood when Deb recounted an interesting encounter she had with a woman from Texas who had come to Louisville to visit her mother's hometown. The elderly woman had recently died, and before she did so, she made a compelling deathbed confession that tugged at the daughter's heart strings and prompted the Louisville visit.

It seems that long before the daughter's parents had met and married, there had been another man in her mother's life – a young soldier from Kentucky. Even though she had loved the girl's father dearly, this man had been "the one true love of her life," and they had been engaged to be married. The two had enjoyed a wonderful courtship – one made all the more special by the fact that a last-minute injury had sidelined the young man and delayed his return to Louisville – and he had proposed to her on a bench in Central Park. His family had an engagement party for the couple at 1464 St. James Court, and after the announcement that made the engagement official, a tragedy did indeed occur. The young soldier went to get a new gun so he could show it to a friend, and as he held it out for inspection, it accidentally discharged and killed the young soldier himself.

The wedding never did take place, and, although she did eventually marry, the young girl never forgot her original beau and the wonderful memories she had of him on St. James Court. Shortly before she died, she shared these secrets with her daughter, who – out of respect for her mother – returned to Louisville on a sort of pilgrimage. She visited the bench in Central Park where they had become engaged, she walked the court, and she even went to Cave Hill Cemetery and located the young man's grave. Sadly enough, she didn't gain entry into the home at 1464 St. James Court because the workers she encountered there wouldn't allow her inside. Distraught, she had paid a visit to the Conrad-Caldwell House instead, and found there a kind ear in the form of Deb Riall. Since then, no one has been able to locate the Texas woman, and it appears that the story of the ghostly sound at 1464 St. James Court will linger on like the phantom gunshot itself, somewhere in the nebulous land of half-truths and myths, where lore and legend abound.

Note: Shortly before this book went to print, I got an email from my friend, David, a local history enthusiast and researcher of old homes. When he learned of the ghostly gunshot at 1464 St. James Court he became intrigued and decided to do a little sleuthing on his own and came up with the following information: "In 1946, that house was owned by Herbert H. Moore Sr., an attorney. His wife's name was Zena and they had two children: Herbert H. Moore Jr., 25, and Virginia Moore who later married a Mr. Freeman. The shooting did not actually take place at 1464 St. James Court. It took place at the home of L.A. Hilpp at 203 Northwestern Parkway in the West End. Hilpp was president of the Kentucky Consumers Oil Company. The victim was the son, Herbert H. Moore Jr.

"Herbert H. Moore Jr., born in 1920, was a football star at Male High School and later at the University of Louisville. The Associated Press named him to its 'little All-American' team in 1940. He was studying at the University of Louisville when World War II broke out. He apparently did not graduate. The photo printed in the April 6, 1946 issue of the *Courier-Journal* (Section 2, page 2) shows him in his uniform. He was a strikingly handsome, very dashing young man.

"During World War II, he served in the Army Air Force. A week after the invasion of Normandy, his plane was shot down over the English Channel but he survived. Later, over Germany, he was shot down again and was the only man in his crew to survive. He was eventually awarded the Distinguished Flying Cross, the Distinguished Service Cross, an Air Medal with one cluster and a Purple Heart with one cluster.

"Now come the details of the shooting. Moore was attending a party at Mr. Hilpp's home on February 9. Legend says he was celebrating his engagement, but the *Courier-Journal* article of the following day did not make mention of that. I think it would be odd he'd be celebrating his engagement at a home other than his own, but who knows? I looked for further articles up through February 15 but could find nothing else on the shooting.

"Around 11:30 pm that evening, Moore was accidentally shot by Hirschel Marion Haymie, 24, who lived at 1914 Alfresco Place in the Highlands. The two men were inspecting Mr. Hilpp's gun collection when Haymie picked up a .45 caliber automatic pistol, and it went off. The bullet hit Moore in the right hand and shoulder, then ricocheted into his abdomen. He was taken to General Hospital in critical condition, then later transferred to Norton's Hospital. He lingered there until April 5 and died from hemorrhaging around 7:30 pm.

"It's not known what relation Moore had with Haymie. I suspect they were either high school chums or fellow veterans. As a business owner, Mr. Hilpp may have had some sort of professional relationship with Moore's father, who was an attorney. Oddly enough, Herbert Sr., passed away just two weeks and one day later at his home on St. James Court, on April 20 at 8:20 pm. The *Courier-Journal* gave only basic information about his death.

"Sometime after the double deaths, Zena Moore sold the house at 1464 St. James Court and apparently moved out of Louisville. There's a Virginia Moore shown as living on Anderson Street in the 1949 city directory, but after a cursory examination of a few city directories between 1949 and 1969, I could find no Zena Moore in Louisville. Zena Moore died in January 1969. Virginia

Moore Freeman died in late July or early August 1976. The *Courier-Journal* did not have any death notices for either one, which indicates to me they were probably living elsewhere at the time of their deaths.

"Herbert Moore Sr.; Herbert Moore Jr.; Zena Moore; and Virginia Moore Freeman are all buried at Section 30, Lot 139 at Cave Hill Cemetery. I found their tombstone, which is near the Grinstead Drive entrance. According to the tombstone, Mr. Moore Sr. was 56 or 57 at the time of his death (1889-1946). The *Courier-Journal* erroneously said he was 55. Mr. Moore Jr. was 25 (1920-1946). Zena Moore was about 73 when she died (1896-1969).Virginia Moore Freeman was about 58 when she died (1918-1976). I think my only question is about the father's death. It's noted he died on April 20 at 8:20 pm, which is around the time that people say they have heard a gunshot. The *Courier-Journal* did not give a cause of death, so how did he die?"

It's wild speculation, but did Mr. Moore Sr., kill himself? His son was buried on April 8, just 12 days earlier. In his grief, did he decide to just end it all? And so the gunshot that's heard – maybe it's not the single shot that killed the son, but perhaps one that resulted in the father's death? Who knows? We'll have to wait and see until someone can locate a copy of the original death certificate for Mr. Moore Sr. in Frankfort and determine the actual cause of death. Until then, the mystery surrounding 1464 St. James Court will linger on like the sound of the ghostly gunshot at 1464 St. James Court.

ABOUT THE OLD MARINE HOSPITAL

In 1837, as steamboats churned up and down American waterways and established their dominance over riparian traffic, Congress authorized the construction of a state-of-the-art U.S. Marine Hospital in Louisville to benefit "sick seamen, boatmen, and other navigators on the western rivers and lakes." For the young country, these "western rivers and lakes" referred primarily to the

Ohio and Mississippi River systems, and the Great Lakes, where steamboats had emerged as the major factor in the growth and development of industry.

Louisville's hospital would serve as a prototype for a total of seven such facilities, including those in Natchez, Mississippi; Paducah, Kentucky; St. Louis, Missouri; Napoleon, Arkansas; Wheeling, West Virginia; and Cleveland, Ohio, that Congress had funded to address the pressing health needs of boatmen on the Western rivers and lakes. Although many considered the life of the boatman an exciting and adventurous one, the sailors often worked jobs fraught with danger and peril, and diseases such as typhoid, cholera, yellow fever and smallpox brought on by exposure to climatic extremes claimed many victims. If they escaped injuries due to wrecks, boiler explosions and loading accidents, they had a good chance of succumbing to other perils ever present in the rough-and-tumble ports they frequented: violence, alcoholism and social diseases.

The Louisville site, halfway between the downtown and the Portland wharves, had been selected, naturally, for the pleasant views of the water it afforded, and "the impressions and associations it would naturally awake in the minds of men whose occupation were so intimately connected with it." Robert Mills, America's first native-born professional architect, designed the three-story building in modified Greek revival style, and construction took place between 1845 and 1852. After more than 120 years in service, the hospital closed down in 1975 and has been vacant ever since. There are those who believe, nonetheless, that some phantoms of the past have not abandoned ship and still roam the halls of this commanding structure, the last of the original marine hospital structures in the nation.

"I was involved in a recent restoration project there," explains Tim Woods, a native of Louisville who experienced a series of odd events in the old hospital in 2004, "and that place really spooked me at times." Woods had been employed as a painter after the Kentucky Humanities Council awarded a grant that allowed for the restoration of four rooms that would serve as display areas and meeting spaces, while hospital supporters kicked off fund-raising efforts to save the old structure that had been placed on the National Trust for Historic Preservation's list of the country's 11 Most Endangered Buildings.

"It all started one day when I heard this weird whistling coming down one of the hallways," he recalls. "It sounded like someone was walking down the hall and whistling a kind of sailing tune or something. I didn't think anything of it until I remembered that all the others had gone on their lunch break and that I was the only one there. I went and checked to see if anyone had stayed behind, and there was no one at all." On another occasion several days later, the young painter claims he had a rather disconcerting encounter with something that appeared to be "an old-fashioned sailor." This time, he says, a coworker had been present to experience the strange occurrence, so any questions he harbored as to the accuracy of his initial encounter with the whistling ghost were soon erased.

"Now, if you ask my buddy who was there that day, he'll swear up and down it didn't happen, because he's afraid people will laugh at him. But I know better," Woods says. "I don't go around and tell everyone I see about the strange things that went on in that place, but I'm not going to deny it, either. I guess I have enough strength in my own convictions to know what I believe and what I saw, and I don't pay no never-mind to whether people believe me or not." He may enjoy the strength of his own convictions; however, Woods readily concedes that he most likely wouldn't have believed other individuals had they recounted the same stories he tells about his odd experiences at the old marine hospital.

"What happened was this: We were both in the same hallway where I had heard that strange whistling – on several occasions by that point – and we were making our way out to one of the galleries where we could take a smoke break. And we were sort of riled up anyhow because we both kept getting the feeling that somebody was watching us in the room where we were painting. My buddy just spun around all of a sudden and yelled at me, complaining that he wanted me to stop staring at him. I told him that I had been concentrating on my work, but he wouldn't believe me till he saw with his own two eyes that I was facing the wall and not looking at him when he still kept getting the same weird feelings.

"So we stepped out onto the gallery and lit up our cigarettes, and it just got all weird all of a sudden. The hair stood up on our necks, and the whole place just felt all staticky and like it was charged with energy or something. It got real cold, too, just like an icy wind blew in, and when that happened, my buddy just sort of looked at me as if to ask what was going on. He was standing and looking out at the river, and I had my back to it, and suddenly I could tell he saw something, because his eyes got all big and wide. I turned a little to see what had caught his attention, and there, right next to me, was this man!

"All I could come up with is that he was an old-time sailor or something. He had on tight, striped pants and a short jacket and a straw hat. It definitely wasn't anything you'd see men wearing nowadays. I couldn't believe my eyes and I'm sure my friend almost fainted, he looked so scared. But before anything could happen, the guy just disappeared. I don't even think he realized we were there. He just sort of appeared for a moment or two, and then was gone. Maybe he wasn't even alive, I don't know. It was almost like we were seeing an old-fashioned picture. It was weird, that's all I know.

"Well, my buddy hightailed it back inside, and when I tried to talk to him about it, he just said he didn't believe in that kind of thing, and he wouldn't admit to seeing anything at all. Although, like I said, I know he saw it just by the reaction he gave and the look on his face. He was kind of a religious type and he would only say that ghosts and such things were evil and of the Devil. There were several times when I know he heard the whistling as well, but he always tried to ignore it. I could tell, though, that he could hear it, because he would get all tense and red in the face, just like he was doing his darndest to pretend it wasn't happening!

"That's his problem, though, and not mine," says Woods. "If he doesn't want to acknowledge it, that's his prerogative, I guess. I never could understand people like that, though. There's so much out there we human beings don't have a clue about, and there's nothing wrong in keeping an open mind about things. What else can you do? I'm not the kind who can stick my head in the sand and pretend that things aren't happening when they are happening!"

It appears that Louisville's U.S. Marine Hospital, a national landmark and a local treasure, is a "happening" place in more ways than one. Workers recently began a total renovation of the imposing brick structure in one of Louisville's oldest neighborhoods and hope to have it completely restored to its former glory one day soon. More than one worker has reported the mysterious sound of a man whistling in the empty hallways and vacant galleries when no one has been there; yet others have detailed accounts of eerie encounters with shadow-like figures darting down the musty corridors and misty forms that hover effortlessly above the time-worn floors. Disembodied voices like songs from the mariner past echo through the deserted wards where only phantoms and memories languish, blurring the fine line between the Here and Now and the There and Then.

Information courtesy of U.S. Marine Hospital Online
http://www.marinehospital.org/

Chapter 6

1135 SOUTH FIRST STREET

large, brick structure with white trim and an imposing tower looms over the 1100 block of South First Street. Small, dormered windows accented in burgundy-red peer down over the neighborhood from the pyramidal roof overhead. With its austere façade, four stories and the solid, turret-like addition jutting skywards, it cuts a rather striking, albeit somewhat daunting, figure from the street level. And, when the occasional fog swells up from the Ohio River and rolls in to blanket the neighborhood in a billowy shroud of milky white, it joins the ranks of church steeples and bell towers that rise like needles above the dense haze and pierce the low-hanging sky over Old Louisville. Although it sits tucked away on a block seldom seen by visitors, it commands attention nonetheless and jealously guards its spot in local history. Like most old buildings in Old Louisville, 1135 South First Street has seen numerous past lives, and even though time has rubbed the slate of memory clean for many, the staid old home harbors untold secrets and a disembodied spirit or two.

"The first time I saw the ghost, I almost fell over from

shock," says Babette Philips. A recent graduate of Bellarmine University, the 20-something lived in the large building for more than three years. When she moved into the spacious condo on the second floor, she never expected her quarters to come with its own ghost. "If anyone had told me that they had seen the strange things I saw in that building, I wouldn't have believed them. I've always considered myself *extremely* skeptical of things like this, so when you actually experience a paranormal occurrence, it's quite a shock. And, when the shoe's on the other foot, it really makes you stop and think. I'm a true believer now, but I don't expect people to believe it when I tell them I saw a ghost. And, I really don't care, to tell you the truth, because I know what I saw, and that's all I need."

Babette's friends, on the other hand, told her that what she really needed was an exorcist.

It seems that once she saw the ghost, it grew attached to her and refused to leave the premises. "I had been there for about a half year when I saw the ghost for the first time, and I had pretty much settled in and had everything unpacked and in its place. But I kept misplacing things, and it was starting to get on my nerves," she recalls. "I just assumed it was because I wasn't used to the layout of the apartment and was being forgetful, but then little things started to happen that made me think that maybe I wasn't being so forgetful after all." For example, when she would go to bed at night and place her glasses on the nightstand next to her side of the bed, she would awake the next morning to find that they had been placed on the nightstand on the *other* side of the bed. "The first time it happened, I figured I must have put them there before I went to bed or something, because there's no way I would reach all the away across my king-size bed and put them on the table farthest away from me," Philips explains. "But when it kept happening over and over again, I knew something was up. Someone or *something* was moving my glasses to the other side of the bed while I slept. I always read before I fall asleep, and the last thing I do before turning out the light is put my glasses down next to my book on the nightstand."

Not only that, Philips claims an unseen force started to open and close doors in the various rooms of the condominium. "One

*A comfortable condominium building today, the imposing
structure at 1135 South First Street harbors a ghostly secret.*

day, I had just come out of the bathroom and walked into my bedroom when I suddenly heard a loud *slam!* coming from the living
room. I ran out to see what it was, and it turned out to be the door
leading into the guest bedroom." Mesmerized by the sight unfold-
ing before her, Philips says she stared on in amazement as the door
opened and then slammed shut with a loud bang *three times in a
row.* "Now, when it happens over and over like that, you know it
cannot be the wind," she explains. "Something had to actually pull
the door open each time and then slam it shut. And I know I was-
n't imagining that!"

On another occasion, loud noises drew the startled woman
to the kitchen. "It sounded like someone was in the kitchen putting
things away or something because I could hear the cupboard doors
opening and closing, and it sounded like someone was pulling open
the drawers and closing them. But they kept doing it over and over
again. That's what made me nervous." Somewhat apprehensively,
the young lady approached the entryway to the kitchen and
careened her head around the corner, fearful of what she might actually see. "You'll never believe it," she says, "it was like a bunch of
invisible people were in there opening and closing all the drawers
and cupboards! Every single drawer and cabinet door was flying
open and then closing again *all on their own . . .* it was one of the
strangest sights I've ever beheld."

When pressed as to her course of action after experiencing
these initial disturbances, Philips says, "What are you supposed to
do in a situation like that? Call the police? I don't think so! They'd
cart you off to the loony bin if you did something like that. I just
told myself there had to be a rational explanation for it all and decided to grin and bear it. Besides, it wasn't like I was afraid or anything." For Babette Philips, fear would come later on, after she had
her first sighting of the ghost at 1135 South First Street.

"So, this went on for the first five, six months that I was in
the condo. Doors would open by themselves and then slam shut
before my very eyes," she recalls, "My glasses would keep moving
around on their own, things like that. One evening I even thought
I heard a young boy's voice coming from my bedroom, but I con-

vinced myself that it had to be coming from a neighboring apartment or something like that." Not too long after that, Philips said she could perceive a palpable change in her condo.

"It was like the air in the place got very oppressive all of a sudden, very dark and gloomy. And I noticed I started to get depressed all the time. It was like the condo was giving off some kind of bad energy or something." In addition to the bad "vibes" Philips claimed the condo gave off, she reportedly started to experience strange dreams as well. "I guess I dream like any normal person does, but I usually didn't remember most of the dreams I would have," she explains. "But, not too long after the bad energy took over in the place, I started having these really weird dreams – dreams like none I had ever had before." Although the dreams themselves contained no horrific images or frightening scenes, Philips claimed they filled her with a sense of foreboding and despair, and often left her drained mentally.

"Whenever I had these dreams, I'd wake up the next morning completely exhausted . . . *and depressed.* And the dreams weren't really all that strange, because all I would see were these crowds of little kids looking at me, nothing else. But, it was like they were so sad and lonely, and that's the dark impression that stayed with me. All that sadness." When asked to give more details of the children she saw in her dreams, she could only say that "they appeared to be wearing old-fashioned clothing, and they had absolutely no expressions on their faces, just these blank faces with these blank stares." Philips also adds that she could recall very little color from these odd dreams, only differing shades of gray, black and white . . . and sad, pale faces.

When she finally saw the ghost at 1135 South First Street, she would remember these sad, pale faces from her dreams.

"I had just come back from a walk around the neighborhood," she recalls, "and I was sort of laughing to myself because on the street I had seen this old lady they all call the *Stick Witch.* She's always got this shopping cart full of branches and stuff that she pushes around all the time, and there are all kinds of different stories as to who she is – a homeless lady, a real witch, a crazy person who escaped from an asylum, whatever." Residents in the neighborhood have also claimed that they have seen her for decades, if not longer. "Well, I was sort of smiling because she's always very friendly when I run into her, and she always has something nice to say to me. Although, I've heard from others that that's not always the case." Still enjoying the warmth of the spring weather she was leaving outdoors, Philips unlocked her door and walked into the living room in her condo. *Slam! Slam! Slam!* She stood and watched as the door to her bedroom opened and closed three times in a row.

"It was a little creepy, I admit, but I had sort of grown used to it, so I just shrugged it off and headed into the bathroom." She never anticipated what waited for her in the hallway outside the room. "Right there, down the corridor a bit, was this little kid staring at me! Maybe about four feet tall, ten years old or so, I don't know, but he was just standing there looking at me." Philips says she initially assumed that the child belonged to her sister who sometimes arrived unannounced with children she would babysit. However, something gave her the impression that she had just had her first encounter with a ghost.

"First off, the poor thing was all pale and sickly looking. Now I see where they get the phrase 'white as a ghost' from. It looked like a dead child almost. Second – and this is the creepiest part – I realized as it was staring at me that it didn't have any eyes! Just these black, black holes where the eyes should have been. And it's not that he had dark eyes or anything. He didn't have any eyes at all, just these empty sockets."

According to Philips, she and the eerie apparition stood face to face in the hallway outside her bathroom for what seemed an eternity. "I was just hoping it would disappear or something, and it never did, so I didn't know if I should say something to it or what." Finally, she says, the ghostly figure of the little boy turned around and walked down the corridor. "When it got to my bedroom door – which was *closed* – it just walked right through it and vanished from sight." Understandably, Philips, says she felt somewhat nervous about opening the door to her bedroom. "I half expected him to be inside waiting for me when I got up the courage to open the door and venture inside, but no one was there. I guess that's a good thing."

Philips claims she encountered the same apparition on at least five different occasions after the initial encounter. "Things kept moving around the house, and I would constantly hear slamming and footsteps, but the worst was when the little boy would show himself in the hallway," she recounts. "I realized he wasn't a malevolent spirit or anything, but I didn't exactly get a happy vibe from him, either. It was a real haunting, I guess, because I always had a 'haunted' feeling about me afterwards. Those dark slots where the eyes should have been were truly haunting." Although the ghostly manifestation had acquired a normal routine of appearing in the hallway and then turning around and walking through the door to Babette's bedroom, she does recall one instance in which the wraith deviated from its usual habit.

"It was the second-to-the-last time that I saw him," she explains, "and I had anticipated him because the door in the living room kept opening and shutting . . . more insistent than usual." Hesitantly, she turned the corner and entered the corridor to find the ghost there as she had on previous occasions. "There he was, as usual, just standing there and staring in my direction with those awful, empty eye sockets. I could feel the air charged with energy, too. The fuzz on the back of my neck was standing straight up, and an icy chill filled the room. You could even see my breath come out as I was breathing."

Despite the ominous signs, Philips claims she didn't feel threatened by the strange sight before her. "Like I said, I had started to feel sorry for the little guy, because I felt as if he were trying to tell me something or communicate with me in some form, and I decided to try and get a little closer to him. So, I decided to take a step towards him and see what would happen." According to Philips, the ghostly figure threw its hands up and over its face, as if in sheer terror, and bolted away from her. "He put his hands up over his face like he was covering his eyes, and then he ran away. That was the only time I actually tried to get closer to it."

By this point in time, most of Philips' close friends had

heard about the strange goings-on in the large building looming at 1135 South First Street, and many of them urged her to consult a priest or medium who could help rid the premises of the phantom boy. "I didn't want to get rid of him, though. That's what they didn't understand. I wasn't afraid of him, and I didn't feel threatened, so I didn't think it was a big deal or anything." Although she readily admits that the eerie apparition had disconcerted her on more than one occasion, Philips says she had acquired a certain affinity for the young specter. "Yes, all that slamming and the noises spooked me, and, yes, when I saw those vacant sockets for eyes, it did give me the willies, but at no time did I feel frightened for my life or anything. True, I did get some negative vibes, but my gut instinct told me I would be OK."

Her friends, on the other hand, refused to buy this argument and insisted that she entail the services of someone qualified in parapsychological matters. "They were really afraid for me and basically made me have someone come over and check the place out. I *refused* to have a Catholic priest come over because I was afraid that he would scare the little boy away, so we settled on someone who claimed to have psychic powers." Philips knew of someone with purported extrasensory abilities through her mother, and decided to go with him. "Since I hadn't even told my mother any details about my experiences – other than I had seen an apparition on several occasions – I felt reasonably comfortable that this guy would come in with no prior knowledge of the situation. He wasn't a bona-fide medium or anything, as far as I knew, and he was very young, so I was a bit skeptical." But Philips says the amateur psychic quickly changed her mind.

"As soon as he entered my condo and started walking around, I got the feeling that he was really picking up on something," she recalls. "The first thing he did was to walk through the living room and to the hallway, where he stopped outside my bedroom." According to Philips, the sensitive immediately raised his hands to his eyes and held them there for a moment or two. "And the first thing he said was that he was getting a strong impression about *someone's eyes* or something to do with eyes!" Philips says her blood turned cold in an instant at that mention. "I hadn't told *any-one* about the little boy's eyes at all!" she explains. "I was the only one in the whole wide world who even knew that! I was totally amazed when he pointed that out after being in the apartment for not even a minute."

After that revelation, Philips says the psychic entered her bedroom and seemed to walk about in a trance-like state. "Jim – that was the guy's name – walked around in a wide circle and then told us he could sense the spirit of a young boy, and that he used to live in the area where my bedroom was." Intrigued, Philips decided to ask a question of the young medium. "I was just about to ask him if he knew how old the little boy was, when all of a sudden, he just spun around as if he had read my mind and said 'He's young, very young, only eight or nine years old.' Now, you can imagine my shock at that!"

The psychic then continued to make his way through the apartment and reported that he had received impressions from other children as well, but he couldn't give many details, other than "there used to be a lot of children in this house." Within ten minutes he had made the rounds and sat himself down on a sofa in the living room. "I was really eager to get more information from him, but he told me that he wasn't picking up as much as he usually would in that kind of situation. He said he knew there were children involved, but he wasn't getting many details for some reason. All he could say was that there was a lot of sadness involved." Grateful for the information she had received, Philips says the young psychic left after another half hour and some idle chitchat. "He offered to come back and try again sometime, saying that some days are better than others for this kind of thing, but I never got around to calling him back."

I received an email from Babette not too long after this visit from the psychic named Jim, and about six months before she sold her condo and moved to California. "I hope you don't mind me getting in touch with you," she wrote, "but I just read your book *Ghosts of Old Louisville* and checked out your web site www.ghostsofold-louisville.com and was wondering if you knew anything about 1135

South First Street. I've experienced unexplained sounds there, and have also had several sightings of a young boy who I believe is a ghost. A psychic recently informed me that he could sense the presence of a young child here as well. Have you heard about the place being haunted at all? Any information you have would be greatly appreciated."

I hadn't heard anything about 1135 South First Street, so – as I usually do – I got the dogs leashed and took a stroll over to identify the building. As I made my way down the block toward 1135, a wide smile spread from ear to ear as I spied the building that I had seen so many times before. Although I didn't recognize the street number per se, I had always admired the stately building for its squat tower that soared over all the other roofs in the neighborhood. Like other buildings in Old Louisville, this brick structure looked like the kind to have a ghost story, and I was happy to hear that someone had made it official.

Before I responded to the email, I decided to do some research and see what secrets I could dig up about the past lives at the brick giant at 1135 South First Street. Although I had come across an interesting old photo of the building – with an intriguing identifying caption underneath – while doing research one day at the Filson Historical Society, I decided to verify what I knew about the current residence of Babette Philips. I made my way down to the Jefferson County courthouse and began rummaging around in the deed room to see what I could find.

As very often happens, tracking the deeds of the property back to the original owners of the land proved to be a bit of a challenge, so I decided to enlist the help of a friend and title examiner, John Schuler. After poring through aging documents and deciphering the perplexing connections from one deed to the next, he was able to confirm my original hunch: the building at 1135 South First Street at one time had been an orphanage. The caption I had read at the Filson Historical Society identified it simply as "the Old Orphans' Home," but I had suspected that this wasn't the official name of the institution. With John Schuler's help, I discovered that the original deeds identified the property as belonging to the Jewish

Welfare Federation. After consulting the *Encyclopedia of Louisville* I learned that the old orphanage on First Street had been known as the Jewish Children's Home.

I shared this information with Babette over lunch at the Third Avenue Café at the Corner of Third and Oak, just half a block from my house, on a blustery autumn day. The original Jewish Children's Home had been established on December 4, 1910, at 223 Jacob Street and then moved to 1233 Garvin in 1912, and remained there till 1922. In that year, it moved to the First Street location and stayed there until 1933. What was hard to discern from the deeds is whether the building had been built expressly as an orphanage or whether the structure already occupied that plot of land. Although the architectural style suggests an older structure, the deed suggests that two plots had been acquired with the express intent of providing for an orphanage for Jewish children in the neighborhood in 1922. Whether the building actually went up before that year is inconsequential, I suppose, since Babette had a possible source for the haunting in her condominium. Not only that, I had also gleaned from the *Encyclopedia of Louisville* that the old orphanage had also served as a convalescent home for children after it shut its doors in 1933. For more than forty years – till it closed in 1975 – the stately brick building at 1135 South First Street harbored countless numbers of sickly children under its roof.

"That must be why I was having all those weird dreams about the kids just standing around looking at me, with all those sickly faces and all that negative energy," she explained as I divulged this information. "I'm sure being an orphanage all those years and then a hospital for sick kids left some negative energy in that space. There must have been a lot of sad kids around there." Satisfied with the history of the old red-brick building at 1135 South First Street, Babette finished her meal, and we said our good-byes.

After our meeting at the café, I didn't expect to hear from her again.

But, several days before Christmas, as a blanket of powdery white carpeted the entire neighborhood, I got a call from her. "You'll never guess what," she said. "I've got a picture with the apparition of the little boy in it," she gushed. "My cousin was here the other day and she took some pictures, and there, in one of them where you can see the hallway in the background, is a cloudy figure in the shape of a boy. It looks just like the apparition I've been seeing." She wanted me to see it, and we agreed that we'd meet sometime after New Year's when all the holiday hubbub subsided.

Christmas came and went. New Year's was very uneventful, and on January 6 – Epiphany – I went and paid Philips a visit in her First Street condominium. She greeted me at the door with a crestfallen expression. "Come on in," she said half-heartedly. "You're never going to believe what happened. I don't have the picture anymore." I walked inside, and Babette explained what had happened.

"My cousin's sort of religious," she commenced. "And the day she was here and took that picture with her digital camera, she got really freaked out when she saw that form in the picture – and it was obvious right away that there *was* a little boy standing there. But her church teaches that anything like that is associated with the Devil and is wrong, so she got really nervous. I told her not to worry about it and asked her for a copy, and she told me she'd get one to me the following day, so I thought everything was going to be hunky dory." From the tone in Babette's voice, I could tell that her cousin had had a change in heart about the picture and refused to let her have a copy.

"So, she doesn't get in touch the next day, or the day after that, so I call and see what's going on, and then she tells me she's not going to give me the photograph. *In fact,* she had already deleted it from her camera." When I prodded as to the actual reason for not handing over the picture, Babette explained. "She went and spoke with her pastor, and he told her it was an evil photograph that needed to be destroyed, so she deleted it from the memory card and tore up the one copy she had. She told me – all smug-like and everything – that she was going to have no part in promoting the *dark side*. She knew I wanted to show you the picture for your book, too." The distressed woman shrugged her shoulders and sat down. "She never was the brightest bulb on the Christmas tree," she exclaimed with a sigh.

"It was such a cool picture, too," she added. "The image was very clear and looked just like a little boy standing there – just like the little boy I had seen. And *just like the little boy I had seen,* you couldn't see his eyes. It was so creepy. All you could see in the picture were these big black holes where his eyes should have been. I can't believe that *even* showed up on camera."

Babette and I chatted about random things for the next half hour or so, and then I left to go and prepare dinner for the Thursday Night Dinner Club. Several hours later, we all sat by the fire in the front parlor, nursing mugs of mulled wine and hot cider as an icy wind roared outside. As soon as I passed around a large platter of corncakes with bacon and smoked trout, followed by enormous, steaming bowls of turkey and sweet potato dumplings, the frigid temperatures outside were all but forgotten, and we were free to enjoy each other's company. For dessert, I doled out a generous supply of *Happy Balls!,* the locally made bourbon balls that I consider the best out there. With cups of strong, black coffee for fortification, everyone said their goodbyes, gathered their things and left just before the stroke of midnight. As I watched the last of them leave in the bitter night wind, my mind raced back to that afternoon's meeting with Babette, and my skin erupted in a rash of goose flesh that wasn't provoked by the freezing darkness outside. I was thinking about the apparition of the ghostly little boy with the empty eyes.

Just then, the phone rang and almost caused me to jump out of my skin. I answered and waited for the intruder to identify himself on the other end. It was Babette Philips. "You won't believe the visit I just had," she said, apparently unaware that midnight had come and gone. "This old woman came and talked to me, and she identified the little boy I've been seeing." I sat on the bottom step of the stairs in the foyer and waited for her to continue.

"I was out on a date tonight and got back around 10:30," she explained. "I got out of the car and was coming up the front walk when I noticed someone standing on the sidewalk looking up at the building. At first, I couldn't tell if it was a man or woman, someone young or old, whatever; I just assumed it was a homeless person and ignored it." Philips said she then ran the flight of stairs up to her condo, discarded her coat and hat and made ready for bed.

"I went to close the curtains in the living room," she said, "when I noticed this person was still out on the sidewalk, looking up *at my window*. It made me a bit nervous, so I kept an eye out for five or ten minutes, and it became apparent that this person was not going to budge from that spot on the sidewalk." Philips then got dressed again, put on her coat and ran down to face the stranger.

"I went down the walk to the sidewalk, and it was like the person didn't even notice me coming as I approached. When I got close enough, I could see it was an elderly woman, and she didn't appear to be homeless at all. She looked nicely dressed and everything, so I said 'Excuse me, is there something I can help you with?' Well, this startled her because she wasn't expecting me." According to Philips, the woman jumped a bit and gathered her coat tighter around her. "She told me she was sorry for staring, and told me she used to live in my building and pointed up at *my window*. This intrigued me, so I invited her inside, and she readily accepted."

When Philips asked the lady why she was out so late by herself, she responded that she had lost track of time and must have been standing there for two or three hours. "It wasn't that late when she got there, I guess, but she had just lost track of time. She must have been daydreaming." Babette made the woman – a New Jersey resident named Mrs. Weinberg – a cup of tea and sat down next to her as the visitor shared an interesting story.

"Mrs. Weinberg told me that she and her twin brother had both been wards of the state under the auspices of the Jewish Welfare Federation, and that they had ended up in the orphanage in 1929, the year of the great stock market crash. She said she didn't know for sure, but I think her father lost everything and died because of it, leaving them all on their own. The father had a sister out west, supposedly, but they couldn't find her, so that's how they ended up in the orphanage.

"She said they were five years old when they arrived, and things were fine at first. They were treated very well, and – all things considered – they were relatively happy. The only problem was that they couldn't find anyone to adopt the both of them and keep them together, so they stayed on in the orphanage for another three years

. . . until a terrible accident would separate them forever.

"I felt so sorry for Mrs. Weinberg as she was telling me all this," said Babette, "because I could tell it was painful for her to relieve the past, and she must have been eighty years old or so. There were a couple of times when she was on the verge of tears as she told me this. That poor woman."

According to Babette, Sarah Weinberg and her twin brother, Harold, had discovered various nooks and crannies around the orphanage in the years they called it home. "She says they used to sneak up to the tower room and that they had a secret way to get down to the cellar, as well. And they used to hide out in a janitorial closet that was somewhere in the vicinity of where my condo was. I tried to find out where the closet was exactly, but Mrs. Weinberg said she couldn't be sure, but she thought it was in the hallway area somewhere, or maybe where my bedroom was. I guess they had made some changes to the layout since the time she had been here. She did remember it was close to the window that looks out over the street from my living room, though."

With tears in her eyes, the old woman told of the tragic mishap that would claim the life of her twin brother.

"So, she told me her brother had this awful accident and ended up dying from it. But when she told me the exact details, my blood ran cold," explained Philips. I hugged the phone closer to my ear and used a free hand to soothe away the rash of goose bumps than ran up my arm. "They supposedly liked to play hide-and-seek around this old janitor's closet they had discovered, and it got to be their own special little spot, where they would come to when they were upset, or to share secrets and things like that. Well, one day, they both ran into the closet, and they didn't know that the custodian had left a large pail of undiluted bleach in the middle of the floor. The little boy tripped and landed – headfirst – in the bucket of bleach."

"That *blinded* him!" exclaimed Babette Philips. "That's why he didn't have any eyes whenever I saw him. He was blind."

According to Mrs. Weinberg, her brother – although blinded for life – most likely would have made a speedy recovery were it not for one thing: the orphanage had made plans to institutionalize him in a special school for the blind.

"That meant that he and his sister would have to separate," said Philips. "Isn't that awful? When he found that out, the poor thing took a turn for the worse and just lay in bed and wasted away till he died a week or two later. He didn't want to live without his sister and just decided to die instead, and I've got his ghost in my condominium to prove it."

Sarah Weinberg eventually found an adoptive family in New Jersey and grew to be a happy, young girl, although sad memories of her twin brother would haunt her for the rest of her life. After she went to college and married, she made a vow to return to Louisville every five years to visit the old orphanage where she and Harold had known a time of relative contentment and security together. Babette Philips and I hope she makes it back to Old Louisville for another visit to 1135 South First Street.

THE STICK WITCH

Nobody knows who she is, but in Old Louisville there is a mysterious figure known simply as "the Stick Witch." People say she has been around for years and years. She cuts an unkempt, disheveled figure; her hair is wild and gray, and her black-robed body is often spied making its way through the neighborhood behind an old rickety cart filled with . . . sticks.

She pushes her cart noisily over the cracked sidewalks, seemingly unaware of the commotion she has caused. Where she is going, no one can say, and when the sun goes down, surrendering the neighborhood to the darkness, she blends into the night and disappears. Some say she's a bona fide witch who comes to the neighborhood to collect twigs and branches for her fire, but her real home is a small hut tucked away in a nearby forest. It's a dark, secret forest where she can safely practice her magic, and it's magic that makes her a witch.

They say you don't want to make her mad. Should you muster the courage and give her an unfriendly gaze, or should you rudely pass by her without an 'excuse me,' strange things have been known to befall those who incur her wrath. And if you have incurred her wrath, you will know it. A bundle of sticks, bound with twine, will appear on your front doorstep overnight, greeting you in the morning as you leave with a rash of chills that rush down your spine. Your spine will tingle because you will know that you have found disfavor with the Stick Witch, and something bad is going to happen.

Sometimes a red, ripe tomato will fall from the sky and hit you in the head, and sometimes all the cucumbers and red peppers will disappear from your back garden, leaving you with only the most meager of salad fixings. Sometimes your oven will stop working, and in the very worst cases (shudder), soufflés have been known to fall. The only way you can undo these horrors is to curry favor with the Stick Witch and make amends.

The Stick Witch loves sweets, and the most time-honored way of making apologies to the Stick Witch is such:

1) You must wear a black shawl and a straw hat.
2) You must take along a specially prepared picnic basket.
3) Take a large peppermint stick and crush it into many, many little pieces.
4) On a clear, cold night with a crescent moon, go to old DuPont Square.
5) Under the branches of the old trees, form a large circle with the crushed peppermint candy that you sprinkle with your left hand.
6) Staying inside the circle, you must unpack The Picnic Basket, setting the following out on a red-striped cloth:
   1 large bottle of bourbon,
   1 large bowl of sweetened whipped cream,

        1 devil's food cake with seven-minute
        icing, and a *Happy Ball!* for each day that
        has passed since the initial transgression.

7)   In a loud, clear voice, you must cry out three
        times:
        "Dear Witch of Night, please come and feed
        If sweet revenge is what you need!"

Then you may remove yourself from the circle, and rest assured that you are no longer in danger, for the Stick Witch is a forgiving soul. If your oven has stopped from working, it should be fine now, and your garden vegetables should be ripe for the picking.

Chapter 7

ALEXANDER HOUSE

People who visit Old Louisville seem to enjoy two months in particular – May and October. The annual Run for the Roses at nearby Churchill Downs floods the entire city with thousands of tourists during the first week in May, and visitors to Old Louisville can enjoy the wonderful architecture against the backdrop of warm spring weather and animated colors from the azalea bushes and dogwood trees. When the trees have started to flame in crimson and gold and then start to drop their rust-colored leaves on the first weekend in October, mobs of tourists – locals and out-of-towners alike – flock to Old Louisville's Victorian streets for the annual St. James Court Art Show, one of the nation's premier gatherings of artists and craftsmen. Like the Kentucky Derby, the St. James Court Art Show occupies a special place of honor and anticipation on most Old Louisville calendars, and these two events herald their own unique brand of festivities and drawn-out celebrations to mark the occasions. October has become a favorite month for another reason as well – ghosts.

With hundreds and hundreds of well-preserved old homes

and mansions where generations of families have lived and *died*, it hardly comes as a surprise that Old Louisville has evolved as a sort of smorgasbord for those interested in the paranormal. In fact, with well near a hundred reported cases of hauntings in the fifty square blocks that comprise Old Louisville, it has earned the nickname as the "most haunted" neighborhood in the U.S., and October has become a popular month for visitors in search of supernatural adventures. Many opt for a guided walking tour of the area's haunted hotspots while others prefer the enclosed confines of the 13-seat tour bus that whisks them around sites of alleged hauntings in the neighborhood, and it seems that they all have one question in common: "Will I see a ghost?"

But in Old Louisville, visitors have learned to be careful what they wish for.

"I always wished I'd see a ghost one day," reports Angela Barnum of Racine, Wisconsin, "and I love ghost tours and cemeteries, so whenever I'm in a new town, I always make sure to check out the local hauntings." The straightforward, 50-something housewife adds, "We had just spent the afternoon in Cave Hill Cemetery, which was lovely, and that really put me in the mood for a ghost tour. But, I never expected to see anything when I went on the haunted Old Louisville tour. Boy, was I wrong!"

Angela and her sister had signed up for a walking ghost tour of the neighborhood, and I had just guided them – along with some 20 other participants – past several purportedly haunted locales on the eastern side of the neighborhood. As we crossed over Second Street and made our way to a supposedly haunted house on Third Street, I noticed that the two women had fallen behind the rest of the group, and I made certain to keep an eye out for them as the group reached the house in question. Everyone – minus the two ladies from Wisconsin – came to stand before the stately mansion on Third Street, and several minutes passed before the stragglers finally caught up with the rest of the tour. From the expressions on their faces and the way they rounded the corner at a brisk walk, it seemed that something had startled them. They remained somewhat subdued during the rest of the tour, and when the group finally made its way back to the Visitors Center on Oak Street, I was able to hear their story.

"You'll never believe this," exclaimed Barnum, "but I'm sure we just saw a ghost!" Skeptical, I pressed them for details and decided to dismiss their allegations as nothing more than the result of overexcited imaginations till something they said caught my ear. "When we were crossing over Second Street we saw an old, black lady standing on the front steps of one of the houses. She looked like a maid or something."

"Do you remember what house number it was?" I asked, my curiosity piqued.

"Oh, yeah, it was 1453. They had a huge plaque with the numbers on it on the front of the house."

I felt a rash of goose flesh break out on my arms and neck: 1453 South Second Street just happened to be the location of an alleged haunting I had been investigating. I asked them for more details, and the two women explained that they had felt an unexplained force drawing them to 1453 South Second Street as they prepared to cross the street with the rest of the group. "I don't know if it was the house itself that drew me, or what it was," recalls Angela Barnum, "but I felt something pulling me to that house. My sister said she felt the same thing, too, so we decided to run up to it and get a closer look." Standing at the end of the walk leading up to the tidy, red-brick home at 1453, the two women observed what they could only describe as the "ghostly shape" of an older woman – probably African American – in what seemed to them to be a housekeeper's outfit of some sort.

"It was a vague form," Barnum's sister recalls, "and it sort of looked like someone standing in an old picture or something, because it was all in black and white. The features were not very clear, but it was obvious that it was a black woman in a plain dress and apron. We stood there for maybe half a minute and stared at this thing, and then it started to evaporate right before our eyes." According to the two women, this disappearing act had prompted them to rejoin the group they had strayed from.

When I explained that I knew the current owners of the

property and that they had indeed experienced a variety of odd occurrences at the home they had christened "Alexander House" in honor of the first owner of the house, the two ladies could hardly contain themselves as I filled them in on the details.

Kevin Milburn, the co-owner of the house, has lived there for several years, and he – coincidentally enough – has been very active in the annual St. Catherine Street ghost tours that showcase some of the area's most spectacular and most haunted homes. Strange happenings on the premises had already convinced him that Alexander House was haunted, but he was very surprised one day to learn that other people in the area knew about the suspected paranormal disturbances as well.

"On a mid-spring morning in 2004, I noticed a young man standing on the sidewalk outside my front sidewalk gate, staring right toward my home," he remembers. "Curious about his presence, I opened the front door and went outside and asked if I could help him with something." The response from the serious stranger came in the form of a stern question. "Do you know this house is haunted?" Somewhat taken aback by the unexpected question, Milburn replied in the affirmative and enquired as to how the gentleman would know such a thing. The stranger replied that he had known the previous owners and turned to leave. "I won't step foot in that house," he called back over his shoulder. He walked down the street and never returned.

"With that, I knew my odd experiences in the house were not merely stress-related after completing an extensive kitchen renovation," remarks Milburn. "I just added his presence and remarks to my collection of unexplained occurrences I had become accustomed to while living in Alexander House."

Milburn says that he and co-owner Todd Reese purchased this stately Victorian in June of 1998 and quickly set up home, never anticipating that they had purchased a home with a history of hauntings. "Growing up in an old farmhouse, I was accustomed to house noises like squeaking or popping floors and odd tree shadows dancing across the walls and ceilings at night," he explains. "All the things you'd expect from a home that's more than a hundred years

Owner Kevin Millburn suspects his quiet Second Street home harbors a ghost or two.

old. It was character, no more." Or so he thought.

When pressed about his ideas of religion and the afterworld, he says "I never put much faith in the afterlife or where you go when you die. I was raised in a small town, in a large Catholic family, and I was taught certain things about life and death, but I didn't dwell on it." Until unexplained episodes with a distinct supernatural twist forced him to examine his beliefs . . .

"Late fall 2002 our kitchen renovation was moving from plans to reality. First things first, the room had to be gutted. As the demo and removal of debris continued, I carefully planned the new layout and began rebuilding. Electrical wiring was run and the duct-work rerouted. Although I started noticing odd things right away, I convinced myself that it was stress and fatigue setting in, and we planned and executed most of the work ourselves."

One of the first incidents Milburn can recall took place in the basement. "I traveled the basement steps continuously while pulling wires and adding subfloor supports for a new central island. On one trip downstairs, I noticed the basement light switch kept clicking off. I would also feel the hair on my neck stand up and get the strange feeling I was not alone, when no one else was helping me." Although he readily admits that this started to spook him, Milburn kept working. "That's when I would notice how my tools would simply *move* from one side of the room to another while not in use." After observing several items move of their own accord, he says he started to get the impression that someone was having a little fun with him.

"I was running new ductwork from the basement up in the kitchen, and I needed a small Philips-head screwdriver. When I reached down, I found ALL straight heads in front of me. I thought it was a bit weird, but I brushed it aside and found the necessary tool. But when I returned to finish the ductwork, every screwdriver now was a Philips!" Most cynics would blame this on the perfect case of overwork, but Milburn claims that when he turned off the overhead light and started up the back stairs he couldn't turn around because he knew he was being watched. "Someone – or something – was definitely in that kitchen!"

Kevin started doing research on the house and traced the deeds back to the original builders, John Alexander and his two brothers. "That's how it became the Alexander House," he explains. "It appears John and his wife, Rebecca, lived here from 1894, when the home was built, until 1901. It changed owners seven times before us." After conducting more research, Milburn discovered that previous owners had encountered similar situations, and he learned that the commanding general for Fort Knox had lived here in the mid 1930s when Fort Knox became the gold reserve for the United States. "I get the impression that there are gold coins tucked away somewhere in the house, possibly in an old mason jar," he surmises. "But, only the butter knife will tell."

Milburn says that as progress on the house continued, he became very aware of a presence or being. "By now I knew I had a ghost and wasn't prepared to meet it, so I tried to find someone who understood such phenomena and could rid my home of the spirits or whatever they were." He says he contacted a local priest to conduct an exorcism, "which is not done as the movies had me believing," and when that did nothing to stem the flow of odd happenings in the house, he opted for another route.

"A good friend of mine, Beverly, talked me into holding our own séance," he explains. "I hung a large crucifix on the rear brick chimney, the original cookstove exhaust. Bad move. Things went from bad to worse, in my mind anyway. So, I called my sister-in-law, Doris, the only person I knew with the sixth sense." Milburn recalled that Doris had visited the house two years prior to that for a brief stay, and he distinctly remembered her comments about the energy and pull she felt from that rear brick chimney.

"I phoned Doris – who lives more than six hundred miles away – and explained what was happening," says Milburn. "Her first remark was that it was centered around 'that damned chimney' in the kitchen." To Milburn, this made some sense because he had recently finished exposing the brick on that chimney, and he had experienced an especially large amount of disturbance in that area. "Doris and I burned up the phone lines for several nights as I told her everything I felt and how my tools continuously 'moved' across the room, and Doris eventually told me that her name was *Hattie* and that she was an elderly black lady who used to be the cook there many years ago." It appeared that Milburn had "desecrated" the housekeeper's favorite spot by ripping out the original kitchen. "Hattie will go away as soon as you rebuild," advised his sister-in-law. "She's just mischievous and doesn't pose any harm."

Milburn recalls another striking incident that took place not too long after that. "A few days later on a Sunday evening while sitting in the kitchen and staring at that brick fireplace chimney, I once again called Doris," he explains. "About two minutes into my conversation, I felt a bolt of energy fly through me, similar to what a lightning strike must feel like. With that, my cordless phone went dead and I slowly turned and headed for the front door. As I passed under two overhead lights, they began flickering on and off, so I took it as my queue to get out of there!"

Outside on the front stoop, Milburn says he frantically tried to get Doris back on the line. "Nothing! I took out my cell phone, called her daughter and asked her to have her mom call me back. Moments later she did, and when she asked why I hung up, I told her the lightning story. She just laughed, saying she was going to catch the next flight to Louisville." Milburn decided to go off to a local bar for a stiff drink.

During her visit, Doris advised Milburn to alter the chimney as little as possible. "She told me not to cut into it at all, but to rebuild it with the loose bricks and leave well enough alone. She also convinced me to talk to Hattie as a real person and explain what I was doing." Although he admittedly felt foolish, Milburn confesses that he did start to 'talk' to the entity, and, gradually, his mind started to ease – even though the strange happenings still continued. "At least *Hattie* and I were now communicating," he says, "and as the days and weeks passed, the new kitchen took shape. I would let Hattie know everything I was doing, much to the amusement of my skeptical friends."

His friends, however, weren't quite as skeptical when he told them about a visit he received shortly thereafter. "The following weekend the gentleman who saved this house from the wrecking ball in 1978 unexpectedly stopped by." Milburn invited the man inside and began showing him around. "We walked through the house, and he explained all the work that he'd done years ago. When we got to the kitchen, I asked him what the name *Hattie* meant to him." Milburn says a strange look crossed the man's face, and he asked how Milburn knew about her. "You tell me," said Milburn.

The elderly visitor sat down at the kitchen table and began to scratch his head. "She was an elderly black lady that cooked for me and took care of my mother years ago," he responded. "How did you know that? Nobody could have known that!"

"Since that day on, Hattie and I coexist," says Milburn. "But there are times I know she's there, and other strange things have been known to happen. The important thing is that the fear subsided, and curiosity has taken over."

Milburn can now see some humor in the situation and likes to recount the time a famous houseguest of his apparently provoked Hattie's ire. "Lady Chablis, who played herself in *Midnight in the Garden of Good and Evil,* from Savannah, was our houseguest on several occasions," he explains. "Chablis was fascinated when she heard about Hattie, but something wasn't right, because I think Hattie might have been jealous of her. Prior to Chablis' visits, Hattie would always make herself known. There would be subtle door closings, flickering lights or very strong feelings of her being there," he says. "Or sometimes it was more pronounced than that. I remember one night before Chablis' visit I was cleaning the tile floor in the kitchen when a wet sponge flew about two feet across the floor and hit me. It really caught me by surprise, and I turned and instinctively threw it back with a few choice words. Maybe it's territorial, but Hattie wasn't happy whenever Chablis came for a visit."

Although he has never spied Hattie in the flesh, so to speak, Milburn claims that he did experience a strange, otherworldly encounter one day in 2005 as he exited the second-floor bathroom after taking a shower. "I was home alone and heard someone in the hall. As I opened the door, I saw a young, slim-built man standing in front of me. He was wearing period clothing and a long, dull gray coat. His facial features were deep, but friendly. I shook my head in shock, and he was gone." Milburn claims he wasn't frightened, but the sighting definitely "spooked" him. "Who was he and why did I see him, but never Hattie? Once again I called my sister-in-law, Doris. Her comment was that he was a former Confederate soldier who was 'passing through,' and that he had some ties to the home or former owners."

Milburn says the current inhabitants – both from this realm and the next – of the Alexander House have reached a happy medium and have managed a peaceful coexistence. Like many homeowners in America's most haunted neighborhood, Kevin Milburn and Todd Reese have accustomed themselves to sharing their house with the phantoms of the past. And although they have been known to be cantankerous and overly protective at times, they only serve to remind us of the history around us and to add perspective to our place in the present.

ABOUT CAVE HILL CEMETERY

Although it may not be Louisville's number one attraction, historic Cave Hill Cemetery, nonetheless, counts as a popular destination for visitors and residents alike. Designed in 1887 by Frederick Law Olmsted, its shady lanes and tranquil spaces have provided a peaceful getaway from the hustle and bustle of downtown Louisville for over a century. Although once well removed from the city limits, Cave Hill is now an island of quiet and greenery in the busy Bardstown Road area. Famed for its sculpted ladies and mythological figures, Cave Hill Cemetery is truly a city of angels.

Named for the hillside cave that overlooked a small lake on the grounds, Cave Hill was first a successful farm on the outskirts of Louisville in the early 1800s. Prominent local engineer Edmund Lee concluded that the area's irregular landscape was perfect for a rural cemetery, and Cave Hill Farm's transformation to historic Cave Hill Cemetery began in 1848, when first chartered by the General Assembly of Kentucky.

A rapidly growing city back then, Louisville needed a rural location to bury its dead, many of whom died from communicable diseases prevalent in the mid-nineteenth century. Seemingly far removed from the city center, Cave Hill's ideal location and idyllic surroundings made it the preferred destination for much of Louisville's deceased citizenry. For many years, the burial grounds at Cave Hill Farm would be known as the "city of the dead."

The Civil War, however, would see the internment of many nonresidents in Cave Hill when the U.S. Government purchased over 42,000 square feet of land for the burial of Union Soldiers who perished in that conflict. Since then, the National Cemetery at Cave Hill has become the final resting spot for more than 5,000 soldiers killed in American conflicts.

The cemetery would take on its characteristic park-like appearance in the late 1880s when developers consulted famed landscape architect Frederick Law Olmsted about its redesign. Renowned as the genius behind New York City's Central Park, Olmsted had gained recognition as the premier parkmaker of his time. The late 19th century saw a tremendous increase in civic awareness in the United States, and its parks and public spaces became the ideal showplace for this pride. Mindful of the natural beauty already so evident at Cave Hill, Olmsted used the prominent physical features as a backdrop for his grand design. Rolling hills, gently flowing water and virgin forests would share the grounds with elegant mausoleums and delicate statuary art.

Today, Cave Hill Cemetery survives as a brilliant example of 19th-century picturesque landscape architecture. With over 500 varieties of trees and shrubs to enhance its beauty, it also harbors one of the finest arboretums in the country. Fifteen miles of paved roads and walkways meander by grassy hills, countless shade trees and spring-fed lakes populated by all varieties of waterfowl.

Perfect for leisurely strolls or drives, Cave Hill has becomes a virtual outdoor museum that can be enjoyed any time of the year.

One can view hundreds of exquisite works of monumental and funerary art that display a great diversity of historical styles and tastes. Grand mausoleums share plots with small, understated markers, while countless angels and white ladies serenely overlook the grounds. Because of the large number of allegorical figures and seraphs, the cemetery has also come to be known as the "city of angels."

Such notables as George Rogers Clark and J. Graham Brown are among the prominent Louisvillians interred at Cave Hill. The public can also view the gravesites of Jim Porter, the Kentucky Giant, and Patty Hill, author of the "Happy Birthday" song.

The most frequently visited plot in Cave Hill Cemetery, without a doubt, belongs to Colonel Harland Sanders, philanthropist and fried chicken magnate. A solid yellow line painted on the road leads the throngs of visitors to his monument, which includes a bust of the Colonel sculpted by his daughter, Margaret.

Cave Hill is open every day of the year, weather permitting, from 8:00 a.m. to 4:45 p.m. Although the public is encouraged to enjoy its walkways and park-like atmosphere, caretakers remind visitors that Cave Hill is first and foremost a cemetery. Jogging and picnicking are not allowed, and guests are requested to be mindful of their surroundings. For more information, call (502) 451-5630.

Chapter 8

THE DUPONT MANSION

any people in Old Louisville have heard stories about the ghost of old DuPont Square, that shadowy figure of a local gentleman in elegant, albeit threadbare, attire who supposedly roams the park after dusk and lurks forlornly in the darkness. Most attribute the sullen spirit to that of Uncle Fred DuPont, a 19th-century socialite who met his untimely demise at the hands of an angry mistress back in 1893. However, local gossip has it that this dejected wraith has been known to haunt other grounds as well – namely those of the nearby DuPont Mansion at 1317 South Fourth Street – and his sad spirit refuses to depart the ancestral lands until his name has been cleared of the terrible scandal that besmirched the family name so many years ago.

One of Old Louisville's most opulent homes, this palatial town mansion went up around 1884 and had been designed as lodging space for the constant influx of DuPont relatives and associates arriving in Louisville for employment in the various family industries. Herb and Gayle Warren took title to the property in 2000 and invested no small amount of time and money in the renovation of the sadly neglected mansion with its towering ceilings, ten-foot windows and doors, elegant parquet floors and sturdy millwork. Workers painstakingly restored elegant details that had faded with time – most notably, the massive hand-carved fireplace mantels of marble and stone that lend the residence an imposing yet stately air – and the mansion quickly reclaimed its reputation as one of the most distinguished homes in the area. Awarded the 2002 Historic Preservation Award from the Louisville Historical League, it thrives today as a comfortable bed-and-breakfast inn with lavish rooms where guests can relax before stealing away across the street for a stroll underneath the shade trees of Central Park, that plot of park-like grounds at the heart of Old Louisville – formerly known as DuPont Square – where the DuPonts reigned over a local business empire so many years ago.

An elegant Italianate mansion of red brick and stone once stood at the center of the park, and Coleman DuPont supposedly used this quiet retreat to hide the body of his uncle, Alfred Victor DuPont, on a cool spring evening on May 16, 1893 while he hatched a plan to cover up the details of his uncle's embarrassing demise. Although the family did its best to hide the specifics of the terrible scandal that had ended the life of one of Louisville's most prominent citizens, many in the neighborhood knew the complete and sordid details behind the demise of Uncle Fred, and so began the legend. But, in this case the legend turned out to be true.

"I had heard stories about a ghost in Central Park before, stories about a caped figure that would be seen roaming the pathways after dark, but I never expected to see him in the house where I was working," says Ronald Haycraft, an ex-marine and local subcontractor who spent several months working in the mansion at 1317 South Fourth Street as it underwent extensive renovation in the late 1990s. "That place was in pretty bad shape," he recalls, "and I had to spend a lot of time there. One night, I was there alone, finishing up on a project, and I suddenly got the distinct impression that I wasn't the only one in that old house." Standing at the bottom of the staircase that wound its way to the upper floors, the 250-pound man experienced something he could only describe as a 'jolt

A perfect example of restoration work, Herb and Gayle Warren's stately DuPont Mansion B&B offers its guests comfortable surroundings – and a mischievous ghost – in a historic setting.

of electricity' that shot through his body. "I had this strange feeling like I was being watched," he recalls, "and then I felt this electric surge pass down from my head to my feet. The hair stood up on the back of my neck, and I could sense that someone was watching me from behind. I assumed someone had entered the house somehow."

Against his better judgment, Haycraft says he turned around to confront the unseen intruder. However, he saw nothing at all, and he didn't notice anything out of the ordinary. "I could see through the door of the stairwell into the entry hall, but there wasn't anything at all. It was very quiet, and I called out to see if anyone was there. When I didn't get a response or hear anything at all, I just told myself I had to be imagining things." But, when the ex-marine turned around to resume the project he had left unattended, a terrible shock awaited him.

"A man was standing there right in front of me," he recalls, "and I swear I almost had a heart attack!" Conditioned after years in the military, Haycraft says his first instinct compelled him "to deck the guy," but as he raised his fist, he "realized he wasn't even real." According to Haycraft, the image appeared very "one-dimensional, almost like a faded photograph in black and white," and "it shimmered and shook as if someone had dropped a pebble in the water and caused ripples that distorted the reflection." The phantom appeared to be that of nondescript gentleman of medium height and build in an old-fashioned tuxedo. "And, he seemed to be as surprised at seeing me as I was at seeing him," recalls Haycraft. "He got this puzzled look on his face and sort of backed away a bit, and then he just disappeared." As he watched the apparition fade away into thin air before his very eyes, Haycraft says he noticed one final, disturbing detail about the ghostly image. "There was a dark stain on the man's white shirt in the chest area, and I thought I could see a small, neat bullet hole."

The startled contractor says he didn't stay around long enough to find out for sure, however. "I just got the heck out of there, and from that point on, I made sure I was never in the house alone again. I told a couple of the other guys who worked there about what I had seen and all, and they just laughed at me and said

I was going crazy. But, I did notice that whenever I'd get ready to leave, no one wanted to stay behind and be alone in the house at all. In fact, none of the guys would stay there alone, especially at night. Maybe they really didn't think I was so crazy after all."

Haycraft's odd encounter, however, counts as just one of several eyewitness reports that suggest that the disheveled ghost of Alfred Victor DuPont divides its time between today's Central Park and the Warrens' lovely DuPont Mansion Bed & Breakfast. Some of the firsthand accounts include those of females who have reported "inappropriate" whispers and untoward advances by an unseen hand, gestures that might harken back to DuPont's well-known affinity for the ladies. Geraldine Beck, a local interior decorator who assisted in the preparation of the mansion as the Bellarmine Women's Council Designers' Show House several years ago, experienced a series of strange events that convinced her of the phantom's rather lecherous disposition, and to this day she refuses to return to the DuPont Mansion.

"I was walking down the stairway from the third floor to the ground floor one day," she recalls, "and I had the distinct impression that a pair of eyes was following me down the steps. I looked back over my shoulder and couldn't see anything, but I still had the most uneasy feeling." Although other people roamed the sprawling mansion, Beck claims she was the only person in the stairwell at the time. "So, I had passed the second floor and was nearing the bottom, when all of a sudden it felt like somebody blew in my ear! And it wasn't a draft or anything. It was as if someone had put their mouth up close to me and blew in my ear. And I could feel the warm, moist air. It gave me the creeps!"

The startled decorator dropped the swatches of fabric she had under her arm, and ran down the remaining steps to the parlor on the other side of the entry hall. "A friend of mine was in that room, and he just sort of stood there and looked at me, because it was obvious that something had upset me. When I told him what had happened, he just shrugged his shoulders and laughed. We asked around a bit, and that's when we learned about Alfred DuPont being connected to the house. He was supposedly a dirty old man, so we decided it must have been him. Not that I believed in ghosts or anything at that point."

The next day, however, Beck said she became a believer. "I was walking down the same set of stairs again, and I had pretty much forgotten about the blowing in my ear from the day before, when I got the same strange feeling. But this time, I actually got a bit frightened. It was spookier than before. And it felt like the whole stairwell was ice cold." The woman claims she continued walking down the steps and had more of a surprise when she noticed the vague outline of a figure walking in front of her. "I could see this shape in front of me, and it looked like a man in old-time clothes from the 19th century. Sort of like a tuxedo coat with a top hat is what I'd say he had on. And I could see a walking stick, too, but other than that, it was hard to tell, because he was facing away from me, and the whole image was very light and hard to make out."

Although she managed to maintain her composure as she beheld the spectacle, Beck says she "lost it" when the apparition reached the bottom floor and disappeared before her very eyes. "I just yelled and threw up my arms and ran into the other room. There was no one there, so I had to go look for my friend, and he, of course, didn't believe me when I told him I had seen something on the stairs. So, I just kept quiet and didn't say anything else about it. But, with all the people going in and out of that house, I wonder if someone else didn't see something like I did."

Beck would have one more encounter with the strange manifestation on the stairs at the DuPont Mansion, and this – like the first – would involve a tactile sensation rather than an actual sighting. "So, it was the third day in a row, and I was going down the stairs again at the front of the house. *You'd think I'd learn my lesson, right?* This time I'm expecting something to happen, so I'm paying extra special attention as I'm walking down the steps, and, of course, nothing out of the ordinary happens. I didn't get any weird feelings or anything, I didn't see anything. Nothing happened." That is, until she reached the bottom of the stairs.

"So, I make it to the bottom of the stairs, and to tell you the truth, I'm a little relieved that nothing happened. I look around the little area at the bottom of the stairs with the nice fireplace, and then I turn and look back up the stairs, when all of a sudden *wham!* I feel this hand grab my . . . *butt!* I spin around because I'm sure someone snuck up on me and was playing a trick, and when I do, the same thing happens. Someone reaches out and *gooses* me again!" Realizing that she was truly alone in the small area, Beck says she then ran from the room and refused to use the stairs for the remainder of her time in the DuPont Mansion. "Fortunately, we were finished in a week, but I don't know if I'd feel comfortable using those stairs again!"

The Warrens and their innkeeper, Mary Ann, happily report that none of their guests in the B & B has experienced anything remotely resembling the unseemly antics experienced by Geraldine Beck; to the contrary, most comment only on their restful sojourn in the heart of Old Louisville and can't wait to make plans for a return visit. If you'd like to arrange a nice escape to Old Louisville, call (502) 638-0045.

ABOUT UNION STATION

A couple of blocks away from the modest brick homes, cozy shotgun houses and frame structures that line South Sixth Street, railroad tracks slice their way north towards the western end of Louisville's downtown business district. Although the heyday of rail travel in this country unfortunately reached its zenith many years ago, countless train stations and railroad depots still dot the American landscape, and the Derby City can lay claim to one of the most impressive in the nation. Constructed between 1881 and 1891, gigantic Union Station symbolizes the romance and nostalgia of a bygone era when Victorians of all classes used a thorough network of railway links to travel through a nation on the rise. The last train from this enormous Richardsonian Romanesque edifice departed in 1976, all but bringing the glory days of Bluegrass rail

A remnant from the grand days of rail travel in this country, Louisville's majestic Union Station counts as one of the city's gentle giants.

travel to a close, but it would appear that phantoms of the past still populate the grand interior, their invisible heels clicking over the ceramic tiles of the concourse as they rush to catch the last train. Destination: *Unknown.*

"I was sitting in one of the old wooden waiting benches that have been here since 1905, when I got this creepy feeling all of a sudden." So reports, Max Kale, a former employee of the Transit Authority of River City, tenants of the old train station since its renovation in 1980. "The hair on my arms stood up all over the place, and I just got a weird feeling like something wasn't right. I looked around and couldn't see anything, but I still kept having that same odd sensation, you know? I went to a meeting on the mezzanine level, and all throughout the conference, I kept having the same uneasy feeling in the pit of my stomach. Sort of like a premonition that something was about to happen is how I'd describe it."

According to the energetic railway enthusiast and amateur ghost hunter, these presentiments weren't entirely unfounded; it seems that Kale would experience something very unsettling indeed. "I've been into ghosts and such all my life," he explains, "and back then I used to go along on ghost hunting expeditions all the time. I had experienced all kinds of strange phenomena, too, but I had never seen anything. That is, until that one night down at the old train station." Although his previous "investigations" of the old Union Station had yielded precious little in the way of supernatural occurrences, the would-be ghost buster decided to follow his instincts and give it another try. "As soon as the meeting had finished," he explains, "I decided to return home, get my gear and return to the station later and see if I could find anything. And by *gear,* I mean the stuff I use when I go on an investigation: a couple of cameras, tape recorder, video recorder and an EMF reader."

Max Kale estimates it took him roughly two hours to return home and collect his ghost hunting items. "I called a buddy of mine who is really *big* into paranormal research," he recalls, "and he decided to come along. We got there about 10:00 in the evening, and since it was high summer, it had just gotten dark. It was hot and humid outside, but the station was nice and cool once you got inside. That's the great thing about these old buildings – they really retain heat and cold." The two men set up their recorders in the spot where Kale had previously experienced the strange "premonition" and they snapped several rolls of pictures before turning on their EMF readers.

"The second we turned the EMF readers on," he states, "We knew something was up, because the dials just went all over the place, and they both made a high-pitched squeal and got so hot we had to drop them." Many paranormal investigators use EMF readers, or electromagnetic field readers, explains Kale, to detect energy that can often be attributed to the presence of supernatural energies. "We both got really weirded out and started talking about it when I got that strange feeling again all of a sudden. And wouldn't you know it? I looked up and saw an apparition standing there. Just as plain as the nose on your face!"

According to Kale, the vision he experienced appeared to be that of a railway worker from a former time. "He looked like an old-fashioned lineman or engineer. He had on striped coveralls with a matching cap and a bandana around his neck. And it looked like his face was dirty or something, maybe with coal and soot from stoking the engines or something. He was carrying something, too, either a lantern or a lunch pail, but I'm not sure which it was, because as soon as he appeared, he disappeared, and we didn't see him anymore that night." Kale claims his friend witnessed the same vision as well, something that they were able to corroborate with a system the two men had worked out for situations such as this.

"When we started doing investigations together," he recalls, "we both talked about what we would do in case we experienced certain phenomena, and one of the first things we discussed is what we would do in the event that we ever saw an apparition." Kale claims that the two had decided they would say nothing at all if they encountered an apparition. Instead, they would both jot down their impressions on paper, and *then* compare notes to see if they had experienced the same thing. "Well, I knew he saw something, because after I saw the thing I looked at him and noticed right away that his eyes were wide open in disbelief. We both grabbed a notepad and pen and started writing things down. After we were done, we compared what we had written, and wouldn't you know? We had both written almost identical descriptions." Kale had described a railroad worker, about 40 or 50, in dirty overalls, with a cap and bandana who carried a lunch bucket or lantern. His friend had depicted a 40-year-old railway worker in overalls with a cap and bandana who carried a switch light. The descriptions sufficed to convince the two men that they had both experienced an authentic ghost sighting.

"We hung around for another couple of hours, hoping to see something else, but that was it for the night. We didn't see anything else at all, and I never got that weird premonition feeling, either," says Kale. "But you know what? The strangest thing happened after I went home and started to go through the pictures and the videos. Neither of us found anything on film, but when we started to listen to the tapes, we got a bit of a shock."

Max Kale claims that when he played back his audio tapes, he came across distinct segments of tape where he clearly heard the metallic screech of engines on the track and other noisy railway sounds, such as train whistles and the garbled din of passengers catching their trains. "My buddy said he had the same sounds on his tape as well. But when we were there," he says, "it was so quiet you could hear a pin drop. We were the only ones in the station and we heard nothing like that at all." Although he did return for subsequent investigations of the old train station, Max Kale says he never experienced anything like he did the night he saw the ghostly figure in the dirty coveralls. He still returns to his former place of employment every now and then in the hopes that the strange premonition that caused his hair to stand on end will once again overcome him, the strange sense of unease signaling another visit from the ghostly lineman.

In the meantime, paranormal sleuths in search of a little excitement are free to go and check out the wonderful interior of Union Station at 1000 West Broadway for themselves. During the day, the public can enter under the large iron and glass porch and visit the ground floor where an abundance of architectural details, including a stained-glass skylight, wrought-iron railings and arcaded walls with pilasters and columns dazzle the eye. Also on display is a rare transportation relic from the 19th century, a beautifully restored 1865 mule-drawn street car, one of only two in the entire world.

Chapter 9

THE J.B. SPEED HOUSE

uring the heyday of Old Louisville's existence, several streets had acquired elite reputations for the ultra-exclusive residents they attracted. Apart from the chic boulevard of St. James Court, many of Louisville's 19th-century privileged class gravitated to the majestic lanes of Third and Fourth Avenues and the shaded walkways of one of the neighborhood's grandest residential thoroughfares, Ormsby Avenue. Much of Ormsby had already been developed by the close of the 1880s, and the 500 block of West Ormsby still harbors some of the grandest – and oldest – dwellings in Old Louisville. One of these – the Speed House – has ties to one of the state's grandest and oldest families as well, and it would seem that some family members still prefer the comforts of the lovely home at 505 West Ormsby Avenue, even though their spirits have long since departed this realm for the next.

Although it still bears the name of its most remembered of inhabitants, the Speeds, the large, sprawling mansion at the corner of Ormsby Avenue and Garvin Place didn't actually end up in their possession until 1893. Built in 1885, the mansion originally housed

Home to the law offices of Franklin & Hance, PSC, the elegant Speed Mansion once served as a hub for the local music scene. Ghostly music can still be heard today.

the family of Dexter Belknap, a local contractor who would leave his mark on many of the neighborhood's early structures. A jumble of artfully constructed red-brick bays and gables with green-shutter accents and a labyrinthine floor plan, the massive house has an airy feeling about it that belies its Victorian Gothic leanings. During its heyday in the early decades of the twentieth century, the structure boasted some 48 rooms and 20 fireplaces, and, although it has seen some modifications to adapt it for its current use as the Law Offices of Franklin & Hance, PSC., the esteemed abode still counts as one of the grande dames of Old Louisville architecture.

As fate would have it, the house would – to a large extent – see many of its changes at the hand of *the* grande dame of Old Louisville society, Miss Hattie Bishop Speed, the second wife of James Breckinridge Speed. After James died in 1912, Hattie, an accomplished concert pianist and avid music fan, had a large proscenium music room built at the back of the mansion in the area that connected the home to the carriage house. Although she reportedly loved to sit at the stately case piano for hours on end while her deft fingers adroitly worked their way up and down the keyboard and filled the cavernous spaces with the music of scales and etudes, Miss Hattie supposedly had the room built for the benefit of the community. "It was a place where recitals and concerts were held," recalls Jerry Lee Rodgers, an Okolona resident, who gave his first piano recital there in 1952 as a budding, six-year old musician. "The chairs were upholstered and very comfortable, and there was a large arch over the stage. The ceiling was very high – 16 or 18 feet – and wonderful chandeliers with alabaster and amber globes hung down from it. It was exceedingly elegant."

Although the stage area has been partitioned off with glass walls for use as a conference room, the music hall still remains in the old Speed mansion. A tiered landing system that allows for added space for desks and bookcases was added later on in the auditorium space, but observers can still spot the pressed-tin ceiling and dangling chandeliers overhead. And the magnificent old piano that saw so many generations of wear at the hands of countless would-be prodigies still stands much in the same spot as it always did, flanked

Ghostly music is often heard in Miss Hattie's music room when no one is at the original piano she used to play so many years ago.

by Boston ferns and an imposing suit of armor. Would anyone be surprised to hear that the old piano has been known to make music on its own, as if played by the invisible hands of some melodic denizen of the past?

According to Judy Franklin, there is a perfectly reasonable explanation for this. The venerable old piano was turned into an electronic player piano years ago when her husband, Larry, and his law associate, Michael Hance, acquired the property at 505 West Ormsby and began renovating it for use as their law firm. She cannot explain the other types of mysterious music she and others have heard in the old house, however. "It sounds like music from the 1920s coming from somewhere between the floors," she says. "We hear it all the time, and no one can ever figure out where it is coming from. Whenever we try to track it down, we end up at a dead

Completed in 1885, the rambling 48-room Speed mansion on Ormsby Avenue retains many lovely original fixtures - and a music-loving phantom apparition.

end." Larry Franklin and other attorneys have experienced the strange sounds as well, and no one has an explanation for the mystifying strains and melodies they have heard.

Although the overwhelming majority of purported paranormal activity at the Speed House seems to involve auditory sensations, some former employees and interns of the law firm have reported unsettling encounters with a ghost they can only surmise as that of Miss Hattie herself. "There's an old black-and-white photograph of Miss Hattie sitting at her piano back in the music room," explains Jane McAddams, a lifelong Old Louisvillian who still lives in the neighborhood, "and she's all dolled up and regal looking, very proud of herself, I'd say. Everyone in the firm knows about it. Well, imagine my surprise when one day I walked back to the lounge area in what used to be the old music room and saw someone who looked just like her sitting there!"

According to McAddams, the figure at the piano had an eerie, flickering, iridescent quality about it that she immediately recognized as an apparition. "I had never seen a ghost or anything like that before – I didn't even believe in them – but the way the thing shimmered and glowed, I knew I had to be seeing a phantom vision or something like that." After a moment or two at the piano, the ghostly form – apparently unperturbed by her audience – got up and slowly moved down the hallway before it gradually faded and disappeared altogether. "I just stood there and watched the whole time," recalls the young girl. "I was totally speechless and didn't know what to do, so I just ignored it and never mentioned a word of it to anyone, even though I had heard lots of people at the firm tell me strange stories about the weird things they had seen and heard. To this day, I'm still skeptical of those kinds of occurrences, and I wonder if I just didn't imagine the whole thing."

Her skepticism aside, Jane McAddams does believe the stories she has heard from others who have experienced paranormal encounters at the old Speed mansion. Oddly enough, many have reported the same type of apparition as the one sighted by McAddams, and all the reported sightings have involved the old music room and the hallway leading to the front of the house.

"My husband had an appointment there one day, and I was waiting in the front hallway for him," remembers Gina Settles of Bardstown, "It was early evening, and as I paced up and down the corridor, I was overcome with a very strange sensation. It was like the whole place became heavy with electricity, and I could feel it in the air. It even made the hair on the back of my neck bristle." Settles then recounts how she turned around and encountered a strange, misty form that seemed to materialize near a door under the main stairway. "I could see some vague details on the face and body, but other than that, it was more of a cloud that had a distinct shape – the shape of an elderly lady in an elegant evening gown." The startled woman then says the odd manifestation glided past her and started to drift slowly towards the back of the house.

"I just stood there and watched her, and it was like she didn't even realize I was there. She floated back to where the music room was, and I just followed at a safe distance. The whole time I watched, I could make out little details here and there, like the string of pearls around her neck and the fur stole she had on. I couldn't believe it!" Settles figures the entire episode might have lasted ten seconds or a little less, and when the ghostly form reached the end of the hallway, it turned left and entered the old music room.

"Now, remember, I was keeping a safe distance, so it took another ten or fifteen seconds before I got to the music room, but when I got there, I couldn't see a thing. It was like she had vanished into thin air." Although the strange form had disappeared, Gina Settles says she then became aware of a faint sound off in the distance. "I was standing near the piano, looking to see where this thing had gone, and I realized I could hear piano music. It wasn't very loud, but it was definitely audible, and it didn't sound like a recording or anything. It sounded like someone nearby was playing the piano." Settles then examined the music room for more clues, and finding none, she decided to return to the front part of the house. "It wasn't coming from the piano that they had back there, so I don't know where that music was coming from. All I know is that, all of a sudden, it hit me that I had just had a paranormal encounter of some kind. I had seen a ghost!" Settles admits that if

An enourmous art glass panel illuminates the main stairwell in the former J.B. Speed residence. Today the impressive structure houses the law offices of Franklin & Hance, PSC.

anyone had told her a similar story before her strange experience in the Speed House, she would have "thought they were crazy. But I guess it's different when the shoe's on the other foot. What I saw in the old Speed mansion made a definite believer out of me!"

Over many years, a similar apparition in the old Speed mansion has made a believer out of former skeptics. Most attribute the ghost to that of Miss Hattie, the former matriarch of Old Louisville society, and few find it surprising that she would haunt the old house where she spent so many happy years. After all, her mischievous, if not somewhat jealous, spirit has been known to roam the cold halls of the stately art museum she established in the 1920s as a memorial to her beloved husband, James Breckinridge Speed, so why wouldn't she opt for the warm comforts of home every now and then? Especially when her old piano and spacious music room wait for her there . . .

As rumor would have it, this is precisely the reason that Hattie Bishop Speed still frequents the venues she enjoyed so much as the first lady of Old Louisville society. Ever the consummate social butterfly, the regal old dame prided herself on attending every single recital and concert hosted in her lavish music room, and a routine soon evolved to mark her presence there. At seven o'clock sharp, she would emerge from the downstairs powder room under the front stairs, and – dressed to the nines – she would walk down the hallway to the music room where she would take her seat in the front row, a gesture that would signal the official start of the performance.

ABOUT FARMINGTON

Several miles from the rambling Speed House in the heart of Old Louisville sits Farmington, the ancestral seat of the Speed family in Kentucky. A graceful, 14-room Federal-style brick manor house at the center of the 19th-century hemp plantation of John and Lucy Speed, its construction began in 1810, and the original design can reportedly be traced to Thomas Jefferson. According to Carolyn Brooks, the director of Farmington Historic Home, this is where William Pope Speed – the father of James Breckinridge Speed – spent many of his formative childhood years. Finally completed by Kentucky slaves in 1816, this historic home counts as one of only a few remaining examples of the earliest Louisville architecture on display today. Most of the structure, together with the original woodwork, glass and brass, still survives in excellent condition, and it has been lovingly restored with original paint schemes, period wallpaper and carpets, and excellent specimens of Bluegrass furniture and antiques from the time.

It has been said that no house in the entire state more gracefully embodies Federal architecture than Farmington, and conspicuous Jeffersonian features include a classically symmetrical design with perfectly proportioned rooms – two of them octagonal in shape – and exquisite fanlights between the front and rear halls. Graceful entryways, hand-carved mantels, and faux-marble baseboards add a special bit of sophistication to the refined interior that would have seemed all the more pronounced against the backdrop of the untamed wilderness that surrounded the estate in the early 1800s. One feature distinctly reminiscent of Jefferson's ingenuity – a daringly steep and narrow stairway tucked away behind an inconspicuous door – seems to be a particular favorite among visitors. The present 18-acre site also includes an intricate early 19th-century garden, stone springhouse and barn, cook's quarters and kitchen, blacksmith shop, apple orchard . . . and maybe a ghost or two.

And not just any ghost, either; it seems that some people have reported strange sightings of a tall apparition in back with a stovepipe hat matching that of fellow Kentuckian Abraham Lincoln himself. Although Farmington Director, Carolyn Brooks, doubts that the well-designed manor house actually harbors any earthbound spirits herself, there are two former volunteer docents who don't share these same sentiments.

"I was walking down the hallway that runs through the middle of the house," remembers Natalie Fields, a Louisville native who worked at Farmington in the early 1990s, "when all of a sudden I noticed someone standing in the dining room. I got to the back of the house and realized that I should have been the only one there, so I turned around and went back to the dining room." But the young girl didn't find a soul when she entered the room. "There was no one there – or in the rest of the house for that matter – when I went back, and I knew I had seen someone for sure. When I tried to recall what I had seen, I realized it must have been Abraham Lincoln, because he was tall and all in black and wore a black top hat like he used to."

Another young volunteer, Jessie Bights, claims she had a similar encounter with the unanticipated vision one day that proved to be a bit too unsettling for her liking. "I had just finished with a group and I had let them out the door," she recalls. "I had some time to kill, so I just wandered a bit through the house and ended up in front of the door with the steep stairway behind it. I reached out and pulled the door open and got the shock of my life!" Before her stood a shimmering apparition eerily reminiscent of Abraham Lincoln. "It looked just like him," she explains, "with a long, black coat, a little beard and top hat. Just like from the pictures."

Although some skeptics would be quick to point out that Abraham Lincoln's towering frame (especially *with* a top hat) might not actually fit in the narrow confines of the compact stairwell at Farmington and that he – contrary to many illustrations – rarely wore a stovepipe hat, especially in the early years, it is interesting to note that the gangly backwoods attorney did indeed 'spend the night' at Farmington. Reportedly Lincoln's closest friend, John Speed's son Joshua had met the aspiring politician in Springfield, Illinois in 1837 when he had received free lodging from Joshua above the store Speed owned. When Joshua Speed returned to Farmington in 1841, he invited Lincoln for a visit as a means of getting over his depression at the recent breakup with Mary Todd, and the future president did in fact spend several weeks there, a visit he would fondly recall in subsequent letters to his friend.

Whether or not the brooding figure of America's 16th president would linger on in ghostly form at Farmington is something no one can say for sure, but it is interesting to point out that his famous specter does purportedly haunt the White House, giving rise to some of the most spectacular tales of hauntings in the nation's capital. Haunted or not, Farmington has borne witness to almost two centuries of local history, and this deserves to be celebrated in a wasteful country that has often viewed its grand old homes as little more than nuisances that need to be eliminated instead of lovingly maintained. Wherever these old homes survive, so does history; and wherever history persists there looms a propensity for shadowy forms and unexplained creaks and groans that might call up phantoms of the past, be they real or imagined. In one form or other, the past is alive and well at Farmington Historic Home at 3033 Bardstown Road. Call (502) 452-9920 to make arrangements for a tour.

Much of this information comes courtesy of the Farmington Historic Home website (http://www.historicfarmington.org/index.html) and Abraham Lincoln Online (http://showcase.netins.net/web/creative/lincoln/sites/speed.htm).

Chapter 10

THE ST. IVES

lthough large, stately mansions and comfortable single-family dwellings dominated the residential scene in Old Louisville, a smattering of apartment buildings and flats still remains from a time when wealthy locals viewed high-rise tenants as little more than residential mavericks with neither the resources nor the common sense to secure proper accommodations. Upper-crust Victorians entertained the strict, albeit somewhat naïve, notion that *respectable* families lived exclusively in large, sprawling mansions with their own grounds and staffs of servants, and anyone who did not adhere to this rigid mold invited the disdain of neighbors and society alike. In the 1890s when the King of St. James Court, Theophilus Conrad, proposed the construction of an elegant apartment building at the mouth of Fountain Court that would reach an unheard of six stories, his neighbors balked and insisted that no self-respecting family would even consider living, packed like sardines, in that can of a building. "Living life on a shelf" they mockingly called it, and they dubbed the elegant St. James Flats *Conrad's Folly* and waited for its imminent demise. Their derision soon subsided, however, when it became shockingly apparent that not everyone shared their same stilted point of view. Around the country, innovative apartment buildings provided alternative lodging for those in search of convenience and adventure, and they offered the additional allure of picture-perfect vistas from over the rooftops. Apartment dwellers came to be viewed as daring, ground-breaking pioneers, and apartment houses offered trendy, even sophisticated, accommodations for both the prosperous middle class and the socially elite. By the 1900s, apartments had arrived *en vogue.*

One of these early 20th-century apartment buildings stands at the corner of Oak Street and South Second Street in Old Louisville. It is a solid, squat building with four floors that failed to reach the heights of many of the city's snazzy apartment houses, but it cuts a striking figure nonetheless. Rust-colored roof tiles, interior balconies and staid exterior tiles with colorful mosaic inlay paint a cohesive picture while hinting at the ghosts of its former existence. Perched soundly on the corner of an active intersection, it has a good vantage point for much of the activity in the neighborhood, and two arched entryways – ornamented with multihued tile surrounds – provide access from Oak Street and Second Street. Unless one stops to study the unique façade, one can very easily pass by without ever even knowing that this building has a name. There, above the entrance and imbedded in a greenish coat of arms, one can spot a handful of cobalt blue mosaic tiles that spell out the name *St. Ives.*

In Old Louisville, many phantoms of the past refuse to leave the confines of the opulent mansions they once called home, preferring the comforts and safety afforded by rambling architecture and sprawling floor plans. However, some blithe spirits have been known to haunt apartments as well. Many consider the St. Ives, for example, a hotbed of paranormal activity, and stories abound about the wailing ghost in unlucky apartment 13.

"When I lived there, there wasn't really an apartment 13 *per se,* but everyone talked about the apartment that used to be apartment 13 when the place was originally built in the 1920s," says Cap Sorrensen, a bank teller who rented from the St. Ives in the 1980s.

"Some said it was on the ground floor, but others claimed it was on the top floor. In any case, different people in different apartments claimed that they lived in the original apartment 13, and that was why they would experience odd things and have bad luck. I never really believed it until I started going out with a girl who said she lived in number 13."

According to Sorrensen, he first got the inkling that there might be something to his girlfriend's insistence that she lived in a haunted apartment on a cool spring day as they prepared to go to the track. "It was Derby Day, and my bank had a box at the track, so we were getting ready to get there bright and early in the morning before the crowds. Even though it was only 10:00 in the morning, we decided to make mint juleps to get us in the mood. I went to the kitchen, and that's when I noticed something very strange."

Walking through the doorway into the kitchen, Sorrensen claims he saw a bottle of bourbon slide slowly across the counter. "It was like someone gently slid it from one side of the counter to the other, a total of five or six feet, but there was no one there. At first, I thought Becky had to be playing tricks on me, so I just laughed and told her I wasn't buying it, but when she looked at me like she didn't know what I was talking about, I realized something weird was going on." When confronted with the moving bourbon bottle, the girlfriend replied with a smug "I-told-you-so." It seems she had told her skeptical boyfriend about various items in the kitchen that had the odd tendency to move about of their own accord, and the bottle of Maker's Mark happened to be one of them.

"When I finally saw it with my own eyes, I felt really bad because I had been giving her such a hard time," Cap explains. "But, it was really happening, and I saw other things move around after that as well." For example, he remembers a strange incident that occurred several days after he witnessed the sliding bourbon bottle on the counter. "I walked into the kitchen, and before I had even taken two or three steps, one of the chairs at the kitchen table just slid out from under the table and sailed across the floor and came to a stop right in front of me." Looking for a rational explanation, Sorrensen says he pulled out a level and checked the pitch of the floor to make sure it was even. "Even if it had been off a bit, which it wasn't, it wouldn't have explained how a chair could go sailing such a distance at such a speed. *Something* besides sheer gravity had to make that thing move the way it did."

When liquor bottles continued to move across the counter on their own, Sorrensen says he tried to look for a logical explanation there as well, but he could fine done. "I saw the same bottle of Maker's Mark slide across the counter a couple of days after that, and I was convinced that the counter had to be crooked or something, so I took my level and checked it, but it was perfectly even." The puzzled man says he even turned the bottle upside down to check for wetness on the bottom that might account for the easy glide. "But, it was totally dry. There had to be some force propelling those objects in the kitchen. To this day, I have no reasonable explanation for how those things would move around on their own."

Sorrensen says he has no explanation, either, for the other strange events he and his girlfriend experienced in their apartment at the St. Ives. "After I started seeing the things move around on their own, other weird things started happening, too. For instance, we started having strange smells that we couldn't explain. Smoke and fire, very often, for example. Once we were convinced that the building was on fire and even called the fire department, but when they got here, you couldn't smell it anymore, and – of course – there wasn't a fire here or anyplace else on the block for that matter." Cap Sorrensen says he and his girlfriend grew accustomed to the unexplained odors and assumed they ensued from a neighboring apartment. "When the strange shrieks started, though, that was harder to explain away."

One fall evening, Sorrensen found himself on the couch watching movies in the living room when a piercing scream filled the room. "It was Friday night, and we were just lying on the sofa while a movie played on TV," he recalls, "and we had just commented to each other that the smell of smoke was especially strong that night. All of a sudden, we hear this God-awful scream behind us, like it's coming from the wall or something." The couple jumped up in fright and cautiously examined the area behind the sofa against the wall. "It sounded like it came from the wall right there behind us, but we couldn't find anything. I wondered if maybe a rat or some type of animal or something had got in the wall and had made that noise, but we never found out. I don't think it could've come from another apartment, either, because it sounded like it was right there next to us. It sounded just like a woman shrieking . . . shrieking in pain. It was awful."

Sorrensen and his girlfriend had moved out of the apartment by year's end – not because of the unexplainable disturbances, but because Cap received a promotion that required him to transfer to Pittsburgh – and they both feel relatively certain that the purported paranormal activity would have escalated to an unpleasant climax. "It wasn't like it was horrifying or anything," he explains, "but you could tell it was going to get worse. When we left, I made sure to tell the manager about the strange things we had witnessed, but he just laughed it off and didn't say a word about it. I told him he needed to warn the next tenants, but he didn't want to scare them off – for obvious reasons."

Although the manager refused to share the information about the alleged haunting with the next set of tenants, Cap Sorrensen had the opportunity to do so himself. "It turns out that a coworker of mine ended up taking over the lease for my apartment at the St. Ives," he says. "I made sure to tell him about the weird stuff going on there right away, but it didn't seem to bother him at all. He just shrugged his shoulders and said he didn't believe in ghosts or anything associated with the occult."

After moving into unlucky apartment 13 at the St. Ives, the new tenant wouldn't be saying that any longer.

"I was always a staunch nonbeliever in ghosts and goblins," says Mike Cunningham, the new tenant who took the apartment from Cap Sorrensen, "so when I heard that I was moving into a supposedly 'haunted' apartment, I just rolled my eyes and chuckled to myself. 'There is no such thing as ghosts!' is what I had always been taught." But maybe Mike Cunningham had been taught wrong.

"The first sign I had that something odd was going on in my apartment happened right as soon as I moved in. My animals acted really strangely in the living room. I have two tabby cats, and they just started acting crazy as soon as we moved in. They were okay in other parts of the apartment, but they got wired up every time they went into the living room – that is when I could get them to come into the living room." Cunningham says his cats gravitated to the kitchen and dining room area, where their food bowls and litter boxes were, and rarely ventured past the threshold into the living room. "My cats always used to sleep with me, but after we moved into the St. Ives that pretty much stopped because it required them to walk through the living room to get to my bedroom, and they just wouldn't do it. Even when I picked them up and carried them through to the bedroom, they'd hiss and spit the whole time we were walking through the living room. It just drove them nuts."

From the safety of the kitchen, says Cunningham, the two cats would often peer into the dark recesses of the living room, oftentimes moving their heads in unison as if following an invisible figure. "It always looked like they were watching something that I couldn't see, and sometimes they'd lower their heads at the same time like they were going to pounce on something. But instead of jumping, they'd usually hiss and growl at something and then run back into their corner in the kitchen. It was crazy."

On other occasions, Cunningham recounts how he would find the two animals perched on the kitchen counter as they faced the doorway to the living room, their backs arched and their tales all bushy, as they bared their fangs at some unseen force and made the most bloodcurdling wailing, hissing sounds. "It sounded like someone was killing them," he explains. "I had *never* heard them make such awful noises before. That's what really made me stop and think."

Cunningham recalls how some of these encounters resulted in what appeared to be attacks the cats attempted on the invisible force. "I remember how – on a couple of occasions – the cats actually jumped from the counter in the direction of the doorway into the living room and looked like they were trying to attack something – or someone – that had just entered the kitchen. They'd scream and hiss and jump up in the air and claw and bite at something that I could not see. Then they'd run and hide in the corner."

From that point on, things only got worse in his apartment at the St. Ives, reports Cunningham. "The cats got so they'd only stay in the kitchen – in the corner furthest away from the door to the living room. And then all the other things started happening."

The "other things" Cunningham refers to included cries and shrieks in the middle of the night, unexplainable olfactory sensations, pushes and shoves by unseen hands and shadowy visions out of the corner of his eyes. The most unsettling of these disturbances concerned an eerie stain that kept appearing on the wall over the couch in the living room. "It started showing up the first time I heard the scream," he recalls. "Some friends had come over for cocktails and had just left when I was making my way around the place shutting off lights and stuff, when I heard this God-awful wailing. Sort of like a woman screaming or a banshee or something – I'm not quite sure what it was, but it was terrible. It made the hair stand up on the back of my neck."

Cunningham says he checked the apartment and couldn't find any reasonable source for the sound. "I just assumed it had come from the street or something." He got himself ready for bed, and that's when he noticed a slight discoloration on the wall near the sofa. "I could see this grayish stain there, almost like it was water damage or something that I hadn't noticed before. I decided to call the manager the next day, and let him deal with it and went to bed." He crawled under the covers and had just started to doze when "I heard that same awful scream again!" Convinced someone had to be in his living room, he ran there and looked around.

"There was nobody there – of course – so I just tried to shrug it off, but that's when I noticed the stain on the wall had gotten larger and darker. I moved the couch and could see that it went pretty much all the way down to the floor. I'd say it was about five feet tall in all, and a couple of feet across." Although he didn't voice his opinion at the time, Cunningham claims the odd shape had a distinctly *human* form. "It was like the shape of a person, but around the edges, it looked all fuzzy and spiky, like rays were shooting off of it. I don't know how else to describe it."

The next day, as the manager of the building stooped and examined the large spot, he scratched his head and looked perplexed. The stain, he told Cunningham, wasn't the result of a water leak or anything, but an oddity that came along with the apartment. "He told me he thought that it had been taken care of already, but apparently not. Other people had supposedly had the same stain in the apartment, in the exact same location, and every time they thought they had it taken care of, it would reappear. I thought it was a new stain or something, but they had been having problems with it for years." According to the superintendent, no amount of paint could keep the odd form from mysteriously reappearing at will. "He said it might take a year or two for it to come back, but it always worked its way through the layer of paint to the top surface. He said it could happen in a couple of months or even weeks, as well."

Deciding the living room needed a new color scheme anyway, Cunningham bought a gallon of paint and had the entire room repainted by the next day. "I bought the good stuff, too, and made sure I gave it three good coats. I was sure that would take care of the problem – for a while at least." He was wrong. The stain had reappeared within a week. "I was stunned," he says. "I had even painted the walls a dark blue color just in case it decided to come back, so it would hide it if it did, but it stood out more than ever!"

Convinced that faulty plumbing or a strange mold had to account for the odd stain, he had a plumber come. "The guy came and took a look at it and told me it couldn't be water damage. Told me it was a solid brick wall and there were no pipes anywhere near it. I checked the apartment above me, and they didn't seem to have any plumbing problems, either. All their pipes were on the totally opposite side of the building, anyway."

When a mold expert ran some tests and told him the apartment had not the slightest trace of mold in it, Cunningham said he was dumbfounded. Although the number of strange incidents in the apartment had dramatically increased since the initial stain appeared, he says he failed to make any connection between the events.

"All this time, I'm hearing strange noises and whispers here and there. Things kept moving all over the apartment," he recalls. "And I'd keep finding wine glasses I'd put in the kitchen sink back on the table in front of the couch; I'd turn around because I had the weird feeling that someone was watching me, and the nearest door would slam shut; the windows would slide open on their own." On one occasion, Cunningham remembers how he turned and saw his cell phone shoot across the living room and smash against the wall in the kitchen. "It seemed like whatever it was, was getting mad at me or something. That's when I started suspecting that the stain had something to do with all the weird stuff going on there."

Not one to let a discoloration on the wall daunt him, Cunningham says he painted the wall a total of five times, and each time the stain would reappear within a week. "It was wild," he says, "and it was like I was getting possessed or something. I'd paint and paint and paint, and then I'd wait and see what would happen. When the stain reappeared, I'd paint, paint, paint again, and then it would come back all over again. I was obsessed with this thing and wanted to win." On one occasion Cunningham – a devout Catholic – says he even walked over to the St. Louis Bertrand church on Sixth Street and "prayed" for the reoccurring stain to not reappear.

But Cunningham finally gave up and decided to leave the apartment. "It was really taking a toll on my cats," he explains, "and it wasn't fair for me to put them through it. We moved to an apartment over in the Highlands, and the cats returned to their normal selves. They were so happy to get out of there. When I saw that, I realized that apartment had to be haunted. Or else it had some kind of negative energy or something, I don't know, but there was something definitely *not right* in that place. I'm glad I didn't stay there." Since then, Mike Cunningham hasn't had any paranormal encounters in the other places he has called home, and he suspects that "maybe there is such a thing as ghosts." He admitted this, albeit somewhat begrudgingly, after I reported a curious bit of information I had uncovered about the St. Ives.

I hadn't actually uncovered it. *Stumbled across it by chance* might be more appropriate. I was out to dinner at Bourbon's Bistro with my friend Kelly Atkins when I approached him about writing a foreword for me. Over a dinner of fried green tomatoes and roast chicken with country ham and red-eye gravy, talk soon turned to the paranormal, and I brought him up to speed on some of the more interesting stories I had come across in Old Louisville.

When I started in about the story at the St. Ives, his eyes grew wide and he immediately cut me off. *"The St. Ives?* Why didn't you tell me you were researching that place before.?" he crowed with indignation. "I can tell you all you need to know about that place. If there's anything haunting that joint, it's my great-aunt Katie Nugent. She died in that place back in 1937." I sat back in my chair, ordered another Woodford Reserve on the rocks, and listened to Kelly Atkins. Several points in the narration caused a fine layer of goose flesh to break out over my arms despite the humid August temperatures outside.

In early 1937 a terrible flood – the worst in Louisville history – rose from the Ohio River and inundated the city in a wet blanket of murky water, mud and silt. Even though more than a mile removed from the banks of the river, the Old Louisville neighborhood saw almost total flooding as well. The majority of the houses, however, escaped serious damage since most of them rest on limestone foundations well above the street level. In other parts of the city, nevertheless, tens of thousands of people lost their homes, and many more were displaced as the flood waters slowly subsided. Kelly's great-aunt, Katie Nugent, counted as one of these. In response to the dire need for shelter, the city supposedly commandeered area apartment buildings to house many of the homeless. The St. Ives was one such place.

"They put Katie Nugent and a whole bunch of others up there," explained Kelly over mouthfuls of strawberry rhubarb crisp. "She wasn't supposed to stay more than a couple of months there, but she ended up dying there before they moved her out," he concluded.

When I asked how she had died and what had happened, he put his Knob Creek down and gave me a comically dastard grin. "That's the part I'm getting to, see . . ." He paused dramatically and

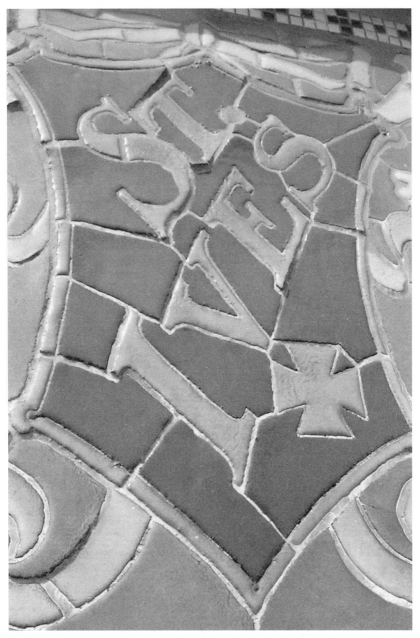

Most passersby in Old Louisville don't realize the colorful mosaic above the entrance bears the name of the early 20th-century apartment complex - or that number 13 is supposedly haunted.

looked around the dining room before redirecting his gaze back at me. "She burnt to death, that's what happened, see?" When he filled me in on the awful details surrounding the poor woman's death, my blood ran cold, because I realized there might indeed be a reason for the strange occurrences in unlucky apartment 13.

"Old Katie liked to sit by the kerosene heater at night with her glass of Madeira, and she'd usually drink till she got tired or passed out. One night, she got too close to the heater and caught her skirts on fire and ended up burning to death. The neighbors said it must have been pretty awful, because they heard her shrieking and wailing, and by the time they got to her it was too late."

The next part really made me shudder.

"And they said she had knocked things over and had fallen all over the place trying to put the fire out, but she finally collapsed and fell against the wall and gave up. They said you could see an exact outline of her body that had been made as the fire consumed her and left its mark on the wall."

Fortunately, we had both finished our desserts long before the story came to its gruesome climax. Otherwise, I don't think I would have been able to stomach another bite.

I tried calling Mike Cunningham to let him know the sad story behind his unlucky apartment at the St. Ives, if indeed that's the apartment he had for a year and a half, but his number was disconnected, and I heard rumors that he had followed his coworker to Pittsburgh for a promotion. Mike, if you're out there, I hope you're doing well.

ABOUT ST. LOUIS BERTRAND CATHOLIC CHURCH

Not far from the St. Ives apartments sits the St. Louis Bertrand Catholic Church at 1104 South Sixth Street. The *Louisville Guide* by Luhan, Domer and Mohney describes it as a structure that "revives a late-thirteenth-century Edwardian English Gothic architecture in the details of its asymmetrical entrance façade, capped bell tower, corner turret, clerestory, buttressed side elevations and five-sided apse." Like many of the old buildings that populate the neighborhood known as Old Louisville, this church made of Kentucky limestone graces the sidelines and does little to call attention to itself. Largely taken for granted – and apparently unperturbed – the stately structure has been content to sit around at the edge of the mostly Irish Roman Catholic Limerick neighborhood and wait for haphazard admirers since its construction in 1873. Those who have the time are free to behold the intricate stonework on the façade and enjoy interior delights, such as the white oak altars, stations of the cross and baldacchino hand carved in Oberammergau, Bavaria. Those who don't have time might see a ghost.

"I was speeding along Sixth Street headed for the university, and I noticed something strange in front of the church as I was passing," says Randall Murphy, a lifelong resident of the Limerick neighborhood. "I could see a hooded figure of a monk walking by, and it looked like he was a monk from a long time ago. It was all foggy out, too, so it sort of gave me the heebiejeebies. I had always heard about the ghost of the old monk who would wander the grounds around the old church, but that was the first time I ever saw him." One of many who has supposedly seen "the ghost of the old monk," Murphy is convinced that what he saw was real. As do the many others.

There happens to be a bronze statue of a Dominican monk on the church grounds, but they say that's not him.

One of Old Louisville's oldest churches, the limestone masterpiece known as St. Louis Bertrand Catholic Church, has served generations of parishioners. The shadowy apparition of a phantom priest has been spotted on the grounds on more than one occasion.

Chapter 11

THE SEELBACH-PARRISH HOUSE

*T*he large brick home at 926 South Sixth Street went up in 1888, an integral year in the development of Old Louisville. The Grand Southern Exposition had just closed its doors the year before after an extremely successful five-year run that put Louisville on the map, and city planners debated plans for the huge wooden exhibit hall that occupied 540,000 square feet at the heart of today's Old Louisville neighborhood. The word had spread across the nation that Louisville counted as "a city of fine homes," and in this year local developers seriously began to bandy about the idea of a revolutionary extension of the city, a new southern suburb that would showcase the finest homes and neighborhoods in the country.

Taking advantage of the abundance of quality building materials and making use of the skilled contractors and trained architects throughout the city, savvy locals poured into the burgeoning neighborhoods surrounding the area that just a few years later would emerge as elegant St. James Court – all in anticipation of the many good things to come. Workers renovated and remodeled already existing homes in the area, and shipments of fine woods, Persian carpets, Italian marble, Oriental bric-a-brac and locally made wall coverings, fireplace mantels, textiles and ceramic tiles started pouring into warehouses throughout the city. A building boom had just started, and everyone wanted to get in on the act.

One of these, a German immigrant by the name of Louis Seelbach, who had arrived in Louisville almost twenty years earlier, built the solid home at 926 South Sixth Street with its unique entry located within a semicircular keyhole opening at a time when his fortune had begun to zenith. Just five years after his arrival, Seelbach had opened a restaurant at the corner of Tenth and Main Streets in busy downtown Louisville, and it quickly gained a reputation for having the best dining in the city. By 1880, the European-style eatery had moved to larger quarters at the corner of Sixth and Main, and five years after that, Seelbach decided to go into the hotel business. He sent for his younger brother, Otto, and the two soon formed the Seelbach Hotel Company and opened a new thirty-room hotel above the restaurant.

In 1888, the year Louis Seelbach built his Sixth Street home, increased demand had led to the hotel's expansion; prosperity reigned, and Louis spared no expense in appointing the interior of his comfortable home with the most modern amenities and splendid furnishings. When a new Seelbach Hotel opened in 1905, the brothers had reached a pinnacle that would ensure their legacy as the most celebrated hoteliers in the city. When he died in 1925, Louis Seelbach counted as one of the most respected men in the state. Understanding this rich tradition of service and accommodation, should anyone wonder that his spirit of hospitality still lingers on in his adopted hometown?

Although Mr. Seelbach himself – and the impressive hotel that still bears the family name – has earned a revered spot in the annals of Louisville history, it appears that time has largely forgotten the Seelbach home on South Sixth Street. As is the case with so many storied structures in the Old Louisville neighborhood, people pass by the venerable old façade, totally unaware of the past lives of the grand old home. Nowadays, renters occupy the spacious rooms of the Richardsonian Romanesque home, and they, too, remain largely oblivious to the historic edifice.

"I had no idea this is where the Seelbachs of the *Seelbach* Hotel used to live!" says Tara Singleton, a U of L student who rented an apartment there in the 1990s. "Since I was an African Studies major, I knew that this is where Charles Parrish lived for many years, but I knew nothing about Mr. Seelbach actually building the house and living here." Charles Henry Parrish Sr., purchased the residence in 1919 and lived there until 1969, and his son, Charles Henry Parrish Jr., gained some local renown as the first African American professor and department head at the University of Louisville. "From the look of the rooms, I always suspected that a very wealthy family lived here. The millwork is beautiful and so are the fireplaces and other fixtures."

I had met the young mother of three at a book signing at Carmichael's Bookstore on Frankfort Avenue, and we had agreed that she would come to my place the following afternoon to tell me her story. The sun shone especially warm for early spring, and I had an extra fan in the kitchen where I prepared a buffet for that week's meeting of the Thursday Night Dinner Club. When the doorbell rang, I invited her inside and, after some brief chit chat, showed her around the house, pointing out specific locations that I had mentioned in my first book. When we arrived in the kitchen, she eagerly started poking around the pots and pans, demanding to know what would be served and what each dish entailed. I explained that I just completed a new chapter in an upcoming cookbook showcasing authentic – albeit somewhat updated – Victorian recipes from the neighborhood, and that my friends that evening would sample some of the test recipes. The buffet would include salmon croquettes with lovage, spring soup, Bibb lettuce with tarragon dressing, Jenny Lind rolls, roast capon with sage and onion stuffing, mashed potatoes and cream gravy, minted peas with butter, lemon chess pie and pecan taffy. After I divulged the menu and invited her to stay for dinner, she eagerly agreed to finish the rest of her story about the old Seelbach house on South Sixth Street.

"Like I was saying before, I was startled to learn who had

lived in that house, but when I started thinking about it, it began to make sense. I gathered that someone who worked at a hotel or restaurant used to live there. It all started one day when I came home and found the kitchen in especially good shape. I am a neat person," she admitted, "but this one day I came home, the whole kitchen just sparkled, as if somebody had polished all the surfaces or something. I know it wasn't like that when I left, and I had almost convinced myself that I was just imagining things when I opened one of the cupboards and then realized without a doubt that something had been in my kitchen. All the cans and boxes and stuff looked like they had been moved around and reorganized! Whoever did this was much neater – and more compulsive – than I, because they had put all the boxes in one spot, all the cans together, and so on, and they were arranged by size as well, so the smallest things were in the front, and the biggest things in the back. Which makes sense, I guess, but I had never bothered to keep the insides of my cupboards that neat.

"Another strange thing happened the next day. I got up in the morning and went into the bathroom to take a shower, and when I came back out into the bedroom, my bed was all made up! Now, I hardly ever make my bed, so I know I just didn't make it and then forget I had done it. In addition, it was super neat, with all the corners tucked in and not a wrinkle at all. I've never made a bed like that! The kicker came an hour or hour and a half later. I had laughed it off and was standing in the room staring at the bed, when all of a sudden, the mattress sank down a bit in the middle, like someone had just sat down on it. Not only that, I clearly saw an imprint that looked like someone was sitting on the edge of the bed!

"Now that really scared me, so I beat it out of there. I believe in ghosts and all that, but I had never experienced anything like this. I've never seen anything at all, so maybe that's why it was so strange for me to see an invisible figure sit down on the bed in my bedroom. I eventually calmed down and came back to the apartment, but the same thing ended up happening two or three more times. It didn't bother me as much, though, since I was used to it by that point. But that's when I started suspecting that someone who worked in a hotel

Former residence of the Derby City's most famed hotelier, the brick structure on South Sixth Street is said to be home to a hospitable phantom who speaks German.

used to live there, because I started noticing that when my bed would be made, the sheet was always turned down at the corner, like they do when the maids make your bed in a hotel. All that was missing was a little chocolate on my pillow."

Although Singleton claims to have never seen an actual apparition, she had several olfactory experiences that caused the hair on her arms to stand on end. On one occasion she returned home from a day of classes and perceived the "distinct odor of German cooking" in her kitchen. "It smelled like someone had just made a big batch of sauerkraut and pork chops," she recalls. "The whole kitchen reeked of it, so I went to the neighbors to see if they had cooked something, and maybe I just got some of the odors. But, none of the neighbors had done any cooking at all. I was a little surprised that they hadn't smelled the sauerkraut from my kitchen. It was an extremely pungent smell."

By the time Tara finished her story, guests had started to arrive. Making herself right at home, she poured herself a glass of wine and didn't hesitate to help herself to food. We sat around eating and chatting for a couple of hours and then retired to the upstairs parlor where someone pulled out the *yahtzee* dice. With an old movie on in the background, we played on into the wee hours of the morning, enjoying the wine and each others' company.

Tara Singleton's stories, although intriguing, wouldn't have merited inclusion in this book alone were it not for the interesting information I uncovered when I started to delve into the lives of the Parrish family, the second owners of the old house at 926 South Sixth Street. I had discovered a Kentucky Historical Marker at the U of L campus that commemorated the life of Charles Parrish Jr., and I decided to walk over and check it out one day. Dedicated by the U of L Bicentennial Committee, the large sign has been installed – appropriately enough – at Parrish Court. One side reads: "In 1950-51 University of Louisville campus was integrated. One African American professor came from Louisville Municipal College, where only blacks had previously been enrolled. Charles H. Parrish Jr., a noted sociologist and a lifelong civil rights activist, became the first black professor at a white Southern school."

On the other side: "Charles H. Parrish, Jr. - In 1959 Parrish became first black department head at U of L, chairing the sociology department. He studied under the noted American sociologist George Herbert Meade at the University of Chicago. His work as an activist yielded friendships with many civil rights era luminaries. This place of gathering is named in his honor." Intrigued, I walked over to the University Archives to see what additional information I could dig up about this interesting man. As chance would have it, while perusing the Charles Parrish materials, I met someone who would prove invaluable both for her knowledge of the Parrishes *and* supposed mysterious hauntings at the Seelbach-Parrish House.

She told me to call her 'Mudgie,' even though her parents had given her the name of Mary Pruitt. A former librarian and school teacher, the septuagenarian had been a student of Charles Henry Parrish Jr. at the University of Louisville during the 1960s. "Those were hard times back then, but exciting," she commented. "Dr. Parrish knew it, too, and he encouraged all his students to participate in the civil rights organizations. We had some meetings over at the house on Sixth Street where we organized for the rallies and picket lines and such, and I loved going over to that old place. It was beautiful on the inside with all this spectacular woodwork and gleaming hardwood floors and the old-fashioned fireplaces. I knew it was a special place."

Mudgie shared some useful information about the elder Parrish as well, facts that opened my eyes and gave me new insight and appreciation for this prestigious local family. "I didn't know Dr. Parrish Sr. because he died before I was born, as I recall, but Dr. Parrish Jr. used to talk about him all the time." According to Mary Pruitt, Charles Parrish Sr., had been born a slave in 1841 in Lexington. He studied theology and became an ordained pastor in the Baptist Church, his political sensibilities giving rise to early involvement in the struggle for equality after emancipation. In 1892, he received no small amount of attention when he registered a formal protest against segregated conditions in railway travel with the governor, and in 1918, he assumed the presidency of nearby Simmons University, a school exclusively for "coloreds." His son,

Charles, received a profound education as a result and carried on the family tradition of involvement in the struggle for equitable treatment of blacks in this country, becoming a prominent figure in the local civil rights movement in the process. Not surprising, the family home on South Sixth Street would evolve as a hub for social and political activism. During a meeting at the Parrish residence, Mary Pruitt claims she had an unsettling encounter with something she could only describe as a *haint.*

"We were all in the dining room," she recalls, "sitting around this massive old table with these high-backed chairs, and we got to talking about different things. The meeting had finished, and we were all just enjoying each other's company. I excused myself and walked to the bathroom down the hall, and when I opened the door and came back out, I saw this strange man walk right past the door. He continued walking down the hall and entered the kitchen, and then I couldn't see him any longer. I noticed right away he was out of place. Not because he was white, mind you, but because he was wearing old-time clothing. I saw him mostly from the back. It looked like he had on black trousers with a white shirt and black vest, and I noticed right away that he had on those thin, black armbands they used to wear on their arms way back when. I didn't get a good look at his face, and I'm glad I didn't, because I fear it might have spooked me.

"Anyways, I went back to the table and sat myself down, and they were all still laughing and chatting, and I waited to see if anyone had seen anything out of the ordinary. They all carried on as if I hadn't even been gone, so I waited a moment or two and then asked if Dr. Parrish had an employee in the house that we didn't know about. They just all looked at me, all quizzical-like, and said that they weren't aware of any. They demanded to know why I asked such an odd thing, and everything went silent. And wouldn't you know it, before I even had a chance to start to explain my predicament, we all heard a series of footsteps coming from the hallway where I had just been. It sounded just as if someone had walked from the back of the house, where the kitchen was, to the front of the house. And, let me tell you, these were very clearly footsteps, like a man wearing heavy boots or something making his way down the hall.

"Well, they all just looked at me like I had an explanation for it or something, and that's when I told them that I had seen a man walking down towards the kitchen, and that he didn't look from this period to me. One of the boys jumped up very quickly and ran to the hallway, and there wasn't a soul to be seen! There wasn't anyone else in the house, either; we were the only ones. So, I speculated that he came up the hall to check on us.

"One of the other boys asked me to describe what I had seen and I did so, and in as much detail as possible. When I finished my account, they just laughed and explained that we had just received a visit from old man Seelbach. I had no idea who that was, and they proceeded to tell me about the German brothers who had built the old hotel down at the corner of Fourth and Walnut Streets. It seems that they had seen him on other occasions, but it was the first time for me. They told me not to be afraid because he wasn't an evil spirit or anything, just that he was an old man who lived in the house for many years who hadn't left the place yet. They also said we would most likely see him again, but that was the first and last time for me. I never saw him again, but I'll never forget it just as long as I live. When you see something like that, it really changes you, believe you me."

Mudgie put me in touch with another local woman, Charmane Willis, who had also experienced several unsettling encounters with the "old German man," as she describes him. We agreed to meet for coffee one Sunday afternoon at the Old Louisville Coffee House, and I was glad to get out, since I had hosted a dinner party the night before, and the kitchen and dining room still looked a fright. My friends, Laura and Beth, both have birthdays in April, and we had just celebrated the night before with a drawn-out evening of sipping and dining. We had nibbled on smoked salmon turnovers in the parlor and then sat down in the dining room. I had cobbled together a celebratory menu of their favorites and we started off with white cheddar gnocchi with sage and gorgonzola, followed by English peas with minted crème fraîche and country ham crumbles. Then came savory saffron-sweet potato bisque and a fillet of Kentucky lake perch with creamed spinach and crab quenelles. After that, we enjoyed coq au vin with spätzle and Chateaubriand of pork with asparagus vinaigrette and wild mushroom ragout. For dessert I passed around lemon-lavender crème brulees, and then came the birthday cake – a flourless chocolate cake with chocolate ganache and homemade raspberry bourbon ice cream. Nursing our bellies, we had retired to the parlor and passed around old photos of previous birthday celebrations as we sipped bourbon and espressos. Although we had had a great time, the kitchen was the worse for wear and would require several days' cleanup. I was still dreading the cleanup when I sat down and began talking to Charmane.

A spry lady in her late 60s, Charmane's family had been associated with the Parrish family, and she recalled a strange incident from many years ago when she found herself alone in the Parrish kitchen. "They were all getting ready for a holiday celebration," she remembers, "and I had run to the grocery to do some shopping for them." Charmane came home and started unpacking her purchases. As she put the groceries away in the refrigerator and cupboards, an uneasy sensation overcame her as she realized that all the others in the house had gone. "It turns out that one of the kids had fallen and hurt his arm, and they had all gone to the emergency room with him, but I didn't know this till later. This was way before the day when they had cell phones and all that, so I had to wait for them to get home before I found out what had happened.

"Anyway, I just assumed that they had run to the store or something like that and went about my business of putting the things away. I had just stowed the last bit of food in the fridge when out in the hallway I saw a dark shadow pass by the doorway. Figuring someone had returned home, I called out to them, but there was no response, so I went out into the hall and followed it down to the front of the house. When I got to the front parlor, it was obvious that there wasn't a living soul to be found in the house because I noticed that there was no car in the driveway. If they had come home, the car would have been there. I even went upstairs and looked around, but I was the only one there. Well, at least I was the only *person* there, because it soon became apparent that *something* else had been in the house with me!"

Charmane Willis says she came to this startling conclusion when she made her way back down to the ground floor and entered the small kitchen at the back of the house. "I froze right in my tracks when I walked into that kitchen!" she remembers. "I almost screamed, but all that came out of my mouth was a small, little gasp." The refrigerator and cupboard doors had all been flung open wide, and all the contents sat in a neat pile on top of the kitchen table. Cupboards and refrigerator had been emptied in their entirety and stood totally bare.

"You'll never believe it," exclaims Charmane, "but every single item had been taken out of the cupboards and the icebox! And not only that, they had taken it all and stacked it in a huge mound atop the table they had in the kitchen. It was the strangest thing I had ever witnessed in my life." Fearing ridicule, the startled woman quickly returned the objects to their proper places and never said a word about the speedy switcheroo she had maneuvered by the time the others returned to the house on Sixth Street. "I've told people about it since then," she explains, "but I didn't mention it to the family at all, because I didn't think it was right. On the other hand, I remember talking to quite a few people who said they had seen the apparition of the old German man who used to live there. When I described what I had seen to them, they said I had surely seen him, too."

Despite their eerie encounters, Charmane and Mudgie have fond memories of the old brick house at 926 South Sixth Street, and they both often find themselves wondering about the current lives of the fabled residence of two Old Louisville luminaries, Louis Seelbach and Charles Parrish. Although they both still reside in the neighborhood, neither of them feels a pressing need to enter the old Seelbach-Parrish House again.

In the 1990s, a local group of paranormal investigators supposedly spent a night in the former home of the Parrish and Seelbach families, and they had some very interesting discoveries to share. Mitzie Rojas, one of the three participants in the investigation, claims the group had access to rooms on the second and first floors of the former mansion, and for more than six hours, they wandered from room to room as they utilized various methods to measure any potentially supernatural energy. Although she perceived no activity in other parts of the house, a clairvoyant purportedly claimed to have sensed a strong male presence in the hallway on the bottom floor, and especially in the kitchen. An EMF reader, or *electromagnetic field reader,* that had remained largely inactive in the other parts of the house allegedly bolstered this claim when it started to register large bursts of energy in the very areas pinpointed by the psychic. Another bit of confirmation came when heat-sensing devices recorded extreme drops in temperature – up to 30 degrees – in the hallway and kitchen.

Rojas claims that the resultant cold temperatures caused the investigators to actually see their own breath in the air, even though the thermometer outside registered almost eighty degrees. The most intriguing part of the investigation, however, didn't reveal itself till *after* the team of paranormal researchers had vacated the premises at 926 South Sixth Street. During the investigation Rojas had been in charge of the recording devices used to document alleged manifestations of EVP or *electronic voice phenomena,* something best explained as "spirit voices" that have been captured on audio recordings.

Interest in this recently popularized technology apparently traces back to the 1920s when spiritualism had reached a zenith in this country. In an interview with *Scientific American,* former Louisville resident Thomas Edison expressed his views regarding contacting the dead: "[I]t is possible to construct an apparatus which will be so delicate that if there are personalities in another existence or sphere who wish to get in touch with us in this existence or sphere, this apparatus will at least give them a better opportunity to express themselves than the tilting tables and raps and *Ouija* boards and mediums and the other crude methods now purported to be the only means of communication." Since Edison apparently held no strong religious beliefs, and he stated that no one could know if "our personalities pass on to another existence or sphere," his statements regarding EVP might best be interpreted as mere faith in the soundness of his inventions rather than a promulgation of the concept of communicating with the dead. Nonetheless, it does beg the fascinating question of whether or not contact with the afterworld is possible.

Mitzie Rojas, no doubt, counts as someone who not only believes in the possibility of paranormal communication, she claims that the dozens of EVP she has captured serve as proof of this contact. One of her most convincing examples comes from the investigation of the Seelbach-Parrish House. After her initial foray into the old residence, she spent several days poring through the formidable amount of tape recordings she had made. Perhaps one of the most tedious tasks of the paranormal investigator, the analysis of possible electronic voice phenomena is not for the impatient as it often requires hours and hours of careful listening and repeated examination of the tapes. Although investigators oftentimes emerge empty-handed from these dull sessions, Rojas claims she recorded several interesting EVPs that corroborate initial findings in the kitchen and hallway. One recording purports to be that of a gentleman repeating the question *"Wo bin ich? Wo bin ich?"* (Where am I? Where am I?) in German. Others include a similar voice saying *"Nein! Komm jetzt!"* (No! Come now!) and *"Gut, essen wir schon."* (Good, let's eat now.)

ABOUT THE SEELBACH HOTEL

When Otto and Louis Seelbach built the magnificent hotel bearing their family name at the corner of Fourth and Walnut Streets in 1905, they must have had an inkling that their grand establishment would one day become the symbol of old-world elegance and sophistication in the heart of downtown Louisville. The massive Beaux Arts construction cost an unheard of $950,000, and it came on the heels of several earlier restaurant and hotel ventures that had catapulted the Bavarian-born brothers to local stardom.

Their newest enterprise would continue a long-held tradition of sophisticated hospitality that would set the standard by which all of the Derby City's grand hotels would be judged, and the opulent surroundings would engender many legends that endure to this day. The two German brothers probably never imagined that they would lend their name to what would become one of the most haunted buildings in the city.

Many visitors to the crown jewel of Louisville's grand old hotels have heard numerous stories about lost souls that still reside in the comfortable rooms of the Seelbach, but the most popular one to date involves that of the hotel's mysterious Lady in Blue. Guests and employees of the Seelbach have reported eerie sightings of a forlorn woman in an elegant blue dress in the wee hours of the morning and other times of the day. People often spot her near the elevators on the tenth and ground floors, and some have even witnessed her stepping into the elevators even though the doors haven't opened. Her eyes red from weeping, she usually appears for a brief moment before disappearing again, leaving no proof of her existence other than the sickly sweet scent of perfume in her wake.

Larry Johnson elaborates this story in his informative book entitled *The Seelbach: A Centennial Salute to Louisville's Grand Hotel,* and according to the long-time concierge and goodwill hotel historian, a tragic accident in the 1930s might account for the sad spirit known as the Lady in Blue. The story has it that an estranged married couple by the name of Wilson decided to reconcile and get back together in 1936. They chose the tenth floor for their meeting place, but as Mrs. Wilson – clad in an elegant new dress of azure fabric – waited for her husband, it became obvious that something had gone awry. Thinking he had changed his mind, she felt devastated when he didn't show up; but her troubled state soon changed to one of utter desolation and anguish when word arrived that her husband had died in a terrible car crash *en route* to the hotel. Filled with despair, she either threw herself down a nearby elevator shaft that had been opened for repairs, or else her despondent condition led to a careless accident. In either case, hotel employees found her body several days later – on top of one of the service lifts. Not too long afterwards, people started reporting strange sightings of the Lady in Blue.

But, this is not the only ghost that purportedly haunts the grand old hotel that has hosted various presidents and assorted luminaries such as F. Scott Fitzgerald and Al Capone. During my years as a Captain and sommelier in the mid 1990s at the hotel's nationally acclaimed restaurant, The Oakroom, I especially enjoyed working in the small alcove, or private dining room, in the elegant, wood-paneled space that originally served as the gentlemen's billiards room. Most Louisvillians have heard the stories about the secret doors and hidden passageways that America's number-one gangster used to make his escape during the many frequent police raids during the Depression years, but most haven't heard the stories about ghostly gangsters that supposedly return to haunt their old stomping grounds.

Many haven't heard the strange reports of unexplained foxtrots and flapper music echoing in the cavernous vaults of the one-of-a-kind *Ratskeller* in the basement, either. Constructed entirely of Rookwood pottery, this unique entertainment space served as a speakeasy during the Prohibition years, and it seems that many former patrons still keep coming back to what used to be the city's favorite watering hole, even though their spirits departed this realm *decades* ago. If you'd like to hear more about Louisville's haunted history during the years of the Great Depression, be patient. I've reserved these unsettling accounts of murdered mobsters and bawdy bootleggers for an upcoming book that will deal exclusively with Old Louisville hauntings from the roaring 20s and the fabulous 30s.

In the meantime, content yourselves with frequent visits to the haunted locales in America's largest – and *most haunted* – Victorian neighborhood and see if you can encounter your own phantom of the past. Keep an open mind, as well as open eyes and ears, as you explore this unique neighborhood and don't be afraid to succumb to its many charms – otherworldly or otherwise.

The phantoms of Old Louisville, these ghosts of the past, welcome you the year round.

AFTERWORD

Once, my eardrums heard a ghost walk, but my eyes did not see the apparition.

Darlene Peppers, a woman hired in 1992 to assist with my mother's bedfast care, one day asked me, "Jerry, do you ever hear anything strange in the house?"

I asked, "What do you mean?"

"Well," she responded, "I know this sounds crazy, but sometimes, I hear footsteps upstairs. Nobody is in the house but your mother, your father, and me, and it's not us."

I said, "Oh, Darlene, this house is getting old. Mother and Daddy built it in 1948. These hardwood floors are old. They creak sometimes. Older houses make strange noises." Darlene replied, "It's not strange noises, Jerry. It's footsteps."

I reassured Darlene that I never had heard unusual footsteps in the house. I said, "I don't think our house harbors ghosts." A few years passed. In the bedroom she designed, Mother died on October 16, 1998.

On November 1, 1999, All Saints' Night, my father fell asleep in his chair in our sunroom. The frail, 88-year-old enjoyed frequent naps. As he awoke, a man stood in front of my father. My father did not recognize the man, who looked forty or fifty years old. The man had dark hair and a dark beard. He wore a white shirt and dark pants from the nineteenth century. The man did not frighten my father. The man merely observed my father. Then, the man began vanishing and disappeared. A moment later, my father told me, "I just saw a ghost."

My father suffered from low blood pressure and an inoperable aneurysm. I reflected on my father's ghost story. I deduced that either my father imagined the ghost, or the ghost represented a guardian angel.

One night a few months later near bedtime, my father and I sat together quietly reading in our living room. I walked to our bathroom to brush my teeth. I heard the sounds of sturdy footsteps in my parents' adjacent bedroom. I thought, "Has Daddy gotten up with his walker? How in the world? He barely can move. How can he walk that fast?"

In the bedroom, dozens of footsteps went clomp, clomp, clomp! "My word! How can Daddy run about in the bedroom like he did forty years ago?" In the bathroom, I felt the vibrations of loud footsteps on the bedroom's hardwood floors. The footsteps seemed like those of my father as a young man when he scurried about wearing leather-soled shoes.

I dropped my toothbrush. I walked to the living room where Daddy sat wearing fabric-soled, bedroom slippers. I asked, "Daddy, have you been up? Have you been walking?"

My father said, "No."

I asked, "Did you just hear footsteps in the bedroom?"

"No."

Chills ran down my spine. I clutched my robe. Turning, I walked through a short hallway to my father's bedroom. I opened the door to the dark bedroom. I switched on the chandelier. Nobody appeared. I opened both doors of two closets. I rummaged within their contents. Stooping, I looked under the bed. I looked behind a wing chair. Warily, I opened both doors to an antique wardrobe. Nothing visible lurked. What had I heard? I heard footsteps in the bedroom, yet nobody appeared present. Had my imagination gone insane? Had Daddy's guardian angel returned? Had a ghost vanished through walls, floors, or ceilings?

My parents, like most home owners in America's past, helped plan, construct, and decorate their own residence. Today, a few years after my parents' deaths, I continue to love and feel close to them. I live in rooms they planned and adored. Do my parents' presences linger in their architecture? A house's architecture reflects individuals and families in personal ways.

Old Louisville presents us with excellent examples of home-owners' designs from the Victorian Period. David Dominé's *Phantoms of Old Louisville: Ghostly Tales from America's Most Haunted Neighborhood* further investigates a mysterious, and, perhaps, paranormal world where erased scribbles on old parchments become palimpsests and where archeological excavations reveal complex discoveries. The world's oldest stories become apocryphal. New structures contain technological marvels presenting questions impossible to answer. Old structures display mysteries impossible to comprehend.

Undoubtedly, Dominé's tales raise questions. Do souls, spirits, and energies linger after death? Do apparitions appear to assist us or to disturb us? Do our five senses reveal all of reality? Do brains have abilities to see into the past and the future? Do future people yet unborn have the capability to visit the past? Can their past enter our present?

The most fascinating question originates in Dominé himself. He freely admits that imagination and legend form integral parts of the ghost story, and although he may be skeptical of many of the stories he has researched, he, nonetheless, appreciates them for their folkloristic elements and entertainment value. His readers should reflect on Pablo Picasso's definition of art: "A lie which reveals the truth" when they evaluate these stories for themselves. Where does fiction cross the line and become reality? I have no idea. To me, each of the tales intrigues.

Dominé's text probes enigmas with no clear answers. Readers may invent theories. As one of Dominé's readers, I feel grateful for his investigation of the paranormal. *PHANTOMS OF OLD LOUISVILLE: Ghostly Tales from America's Most Haunted Neighborhood* encourages my imagination to work overtime. David Dominé, what begot those clomp, clomp, clomps I heard one winter night in my parents' bedroom?

Jerry Lee Rodgers
Okolona,
October 31, 2005

ACKNOWLEDGEMENTS

*O*nce again, I would like to thank all of the individuals who helped make this book a reality, including the staff of the Filson Historical Society, the Louisville Free Public Library, the Old Louisville Information Center, the Friends of Central Park, the library and archives at the University of Louisville, the Spalding University Library, the Conrad-Caldwell House, the Brennan House, the Louisville Ghost Hunters Society, the Dr. Thomas D. Clark History Center, the Louisville Landmarks Commission, Franklin & Hance, PSC, the Information Center in Central Park and the Visitors Center in Historic Old Louisville. I'd especially like to thank Debra Richards, Judy Miller, Marion Wilson, Brian Pollack and Carolyn Brooks of the Farmington Historic Home for their research assistance, and I would be remiss to ignore the huge debt I owe previous writers and historians who have done so much to record the history of Old Louisville. To name a few, they are Samuel W. Thomas, William Morgan, Wade Hall, George Yater, Tom Owen, Clyde Crews and Melville O. Briney. Books such as Joanne Wheeler's *Louisville Landmarks*, the *Louisville Guide* by Luhan, Domer & Mahoney and John Kleber's *Encyclopedia of Louisville* proved invaluable in verifying and corroborating many of the historical and architectural details associated with my stories. As I've mentioned before, storytellers Roberta Simpson Brown and Troy Taylor have been especially inspiring with their many entertaining tales of spooks and specters in this part of the country, and I've gained much useful information and valuable insight from Keven McQueen's well-written books about colorful Kentucky characters.

For their expertise and knowledge, I am particularly grateful to parapsychological specialists such as my good friend Kelly Atkins of Louisville, Starr and Jessi Chaney of PsyTech-Kentucky Ghost Hunters in Nicholasville, Jay Gravatte, Keith Age and the many others of the Louisville Ghost Hunters Society – especially Patti and Bobby Zoeller and Lynn Montgomery – and Cheryl Glassner.

Thanks so much to Troy Harvey, who proved invaluable in helping me design my web site www.ghostsofoldlouisville.com. Once again I would like to thank friends and colleagues, Judy Cato and Jerry Lee Rodgers – both excellent writers in their own right – for their dedication, input and overall generosity. Thanks again to the many neighborhood organizations in Old Louisville for all they do, and for their encouragement and support. I would like to make extra special mention of Judy and Larry Franklin, Joan Stewart, Gabriele Bosely, Rhonda and Michael Williams, Barb Cullen, Jon Huffman, Miss Wanda Stanley, Nore Ghibaudy, Don Driskell, Anne and Alan Bird, Gwen Snow, Anetria Brownlee, Willie "Windwalker" Gibson, Suzy Johnson of the Garrs Lane Project, Charla Stone of Utopia Dream Productions, Deb Riall and the staff at the lovely Conrad-Caldwell House, Ed Turley and the Old Louisville Coffee House, and Jane and Ron Harris of the Old Louisville Candy Company, makers of *Happy Balls!*, the official candy of Old Louisville. To Michelle Stone, my editor, and Paula Cunningham and all the others at McClanahan Publishing House, Inc., thanks again for your continued interest and support.

Finally, I need to thank all the residents and friends of Old Louisville who have opened their homes and shared their wonderful stories with me: Francis Mengel, Polly Clark, Judy Seale, Michelle Dutcher, Norma Ritz Williams, the Calentanos, Doug and Karen Keller, Herb and Gayle Warren, Kent Thompson and Jeff Perry, Dale Strange and Bill Gilbert, Lucie Blodgett and David Williams, an excellent writer who was a tremendous help in proofing this manuscript. Thank you, Mary Jo Harrod, for your wonderful editing skills and also to James Asher for all the graphics in the book. John Schuler, thank you for helping me a great deal with the complicated title searches that opened the doors to the past of so many of these old homes.

For their patience and loyalty, thanks to Ramón, Bess, Rocky, and our newest schnauzer, Edwin, aka "Chunk." Thanks and cheers again to the members of the Thursday Night Dinner Club, some of whom are (or have been) Timothy Holz, Wendy Demaree, Elizabeth Schott, Ramón García, David McHugh, Laura and Mike

Horan, Amber Shaw, Kris Risinger, Allen Land, Gregory Fulkerson, Rick Bancroft, Pavel, Uli Eitel, Joseph Hurt, Big Mary Brooks and Miss Cornelia Sauerbraten. I look forward to many more Thursday nights and many more stories together.